Body Pi

MW00769930

BODY PIERCING FOR STUDENTS

TRAINING MANUAL VERSION 6A

By

Robyna Smith-Keys

B & W Print Addition June 2015

ISBN-13: 978-0-9875065-1-1

ISBN-10:098750651X

This copy is a brief to the point helping hand for Body Piercers. It forms Part of the Australian and International Standards

SIBBSKS505A Provide upper body piercing

COPYRIGHT PAGE

Written by Robyna Smith-Keys Feb 2001

Published by Robyna Smith-Keys

Revised Dates

March 2009, June 2011, January 2013

July 2015, October 2018

Copyright Robyna Smith-Keys

Body Piercing For Students

Table of Contents

Body Piercing For Students

Body Piercing For Students

Body Piercing For Students

Body Piercing For Students

Body Piercing For Students

Body Piercing For Students

Ball Gauge Conversion 176

HEALING TIMES 177

PMMA POLYMETHYLMETHACRYLATE: 179

UNDERSTANDING SUPPLIERS CODES 180

PTFE: 183

JEWELLERY SAFETY METALS - BODY
PIERCING. 186

JEWELLERY TYPES 188

NOTE ON NOSE STUDES 192

SALINE SOLUTION RECIPE 194

STEP BY STEP PIERCING 196

YOUR DO'S AND DON'TS OUTLINED 204

STERILIZATION 209

FINAL TEST 211

7

Body Piercing For Students

PEOPLE STARTING IN THE BODY PIERCING BUSINESS

Hi

Before you begin any of these tests - you must read through this entire book. Then and only then start setting up ready to become a body piercer:-

1. Contact suppliers and gain your brochures and price list.

2. Forms. Set up your forms and number them.

3. Tray set up sheets

4. Procedure sheets

5. Purchase orders for stock

6. Appointment cards.

7. Aftercare sheets for clients

This book will not make the most sense until you have completed your training. However, to read it before you begin your training will without a doubt prepare you to understand your training with ease. For those of you that are already trained in the art of body piercing this book will improve your professionalism.

You will find this manual an immense help in setting up your piercing trays and working through the procedures for each piercing. I strongly recommend you read this manual several times. Be clear on what you are reading and research each section elsewhere as well.

It follows the Australian Standards, SIBBSK505A - Provide Upper Body Piercing and these Standards are approved internationally.

Body Piercing For Students

REQUIRED SKILLS AND KNOWLEDGE

By Order of the Australian and International Standards.

Unit Sector(s)   Sector Beauty

Competency field

Competency field Skin Services

SIBBSKS505A Provide upper body piercing Date this document was generated: 12 October 2012

Approved

A full Body Piercing Course must cover:-

- microscopic anatomy of the epidermis, dermis and hypodermis
- normal process of skin ageing and structural change
- normal skin response to irritation and trauma
- scars, including hypertrophic and keloid (their origin and evolution)
- abnormal scar tissue

- wound healing in different skin types and locations
- effects of treatments on the physical structure of the skin
- body piercing procedures, including:
- preparing service area
- preparing products and equipment
- preparing client and operator
- marking piercing sites
- applying body jewellery
- cleaning and disposing of product and equipment
- maintaining equipment and product records
- maintaining client records
- implementing post-treatment procedures
- implementing procedures for consent forms
- providing home-care advice to client
- appearance of contraindications and adverse effects
- Workplace equipment, product range and manufacturer instructions and data sheets.

The next few pages are only guidelines. This book is not a full training manual and does not cover all the requirements to become a Body Piercer.

You will need to make up your own handout to give to your clients. You will be required to present a copy to your Teacher on the day of your practical exam and practical training days.

This book is: - Exam 7 revision of BP - One at

 Beauty School Books.

http:// www.beautyschoolbooks.com.au

This book is a revision in short form of all you have already learnt. It should also assist people that have been, incorrectly trained to improve on their skills.

Read this book before starting the course. It is a brief outline of the Body Piercing Course and is in no way all you need to know.

Body Piercing For Students

DIY Piercers,

For those of you doing your own piercings at home this is part of my training manual. Have a good read of the sections that pertain to you before attempting your piercing. Never ever, attempt neither a tongue nor an eyebrow piercing at home no matter how smart you think you are. There are blood vessels and nerves that need to be avoided and you do not have the training to do either of these piercings safely. It is always best to have your piercings done by a trained professional.

However if you are a little on the wild side or living in an out back town and want to do the piercing yourself this information will guide you through the procedure. It is always best to have as much guidance as you can possible find. Also, watch some YouTube videos of professionals at work not home users.

There are some simple secrets to a painless Body Piercing

Body Piercing For Students

1   How to charge more than other Body Piercers and have the clients glad they paid you more.

2   How to give the client a painless piercing

3   How you hold the skin during a piercing

4   How you put the jewellery through

5   How you hold the jewellery as you attach the ball

6   How to prevent your client from getting a keloid

7   How to slow down the bleeding very quickly

~~~~ *** ~~~~

CERTIFICATE VERSES DIPLOMAS

CERTIFICATION PROGRAMS

Certification programs are typically specialized in one specific skill or area, which you will study and learn in one or two courses.

These programs do not offer a broad overview of a field or industry, and are often a good option for someone who already has a degree or work experience in the field.

Let us say, for example, that you are a Beauty Therapist with a Diploma. You want to get into Body Piercing because it is a hot new part of the industry, but do not want to go back to school for another degree. A certification In Body Piercing will build on the Beauty Therapy skills you already have, and teach you the need-to-know basics of.

DIPLOMA PROGRAMS

Diploma programs, on the other hand, tend to be longer and more in-depth. They allow you to study a specific area of specialization and get a good overview of the field, without earning an actual degree.

These comprehensive programs are a great option for someone who wants to make a career change and get into a new field. If you were interested, for example, in a graphic design career, a graphic design diploma program would consist of multiple classes that would teach you fundamentals of graphic design, as well as different computer programs and technologies utilized in that industry.

A Cosmetic Tattooist that wants to work with Cancer clients would also need to become a Para-Medic.

For a Body Piercer to have indemnity insurance they would be well advised to also study and gain a certificate in Anatomy

Body Piercing For Students

and Physiology as well as study skin science. A Body Piercer must also have a Certificate in First Aid. A course in -

Para-medical Client care course is always an advantage. However, a Diploma in Beauty Therapy will serve as Body Piercing well. Since 2001 has been listed with the Australian Standards as part of the Beauty Therapy course as an elective course {an add on module}.

Anyone that offers a Certificate in Body Piercing should be offering you at least six weeks full time training. This training should cover:-

Australian Standards, SIBBSK505A - Provide Upper Body Piercing.

1. Sterilization

2. Infection control

3. Room setup

4. Setting up your procedure and protocol book.

5. How to set up your piercing tray.

Body Piercing For Students

6. Practice on non human items such as pig skin and rubber moulds of body parts or rubber faces

7. Practice on at least four humans. But not until you are confident and have been given the go ahead by your teacher.

8. Anatomy and skin science.

For more information on the Australian and International Standards please read this article.

http://training.gov.au/TrainingComponentFiles/SIB10/S IBBSKS505A_R1.pdf

Once you have read this article, you will realize we cannot cover everything in this book. Nor can you learn to become a body piercer in a few days.

IMPORTANT TOOLS

The most important tools for a beginner are:-

1. An Autoclave or a large pressure cooker.

2. Hemostats to hold the ball or the jewellery.

3. Scissors to cut the cannula (the plastic sleeve over the needle) and the bandage.

4. Forceps to hold the skin firm while you push the needle through the skin.

5. A Calliper to measure the distance on the skin, of the entry and exit points to be pierce. Callipers are also used for measuring the jewellery.

6. A measuring ring, to measure the gauge and length of the jewellery.

7. A Refrigerator with a Freezer. (For ice to reduce swelling}

8. Disposable surgical gloves.

9. Sharpie

10.Needle bin

11.Barrier wraps

12.Peddle bin

13. All sterilizing products and equipment.

Note: A Calliper and measuring ring tool can be purchased as one tool as per the photo below.

However, I prefer in the piecing room to have disposable callipers. The joined tool is very handy to have at the jewellery counter for jewellery sales. Customers will often come in to buy just a ball and they do not know the gauge of their jewellery. You can measure it for them and sell them the appropriate size ball.

Body Piercing For Students

Items 10, 11, and 12 listed above. Some may say they are equipment. I beg to differ they are tools of the trade and I will explain why later.

All tools must be of good quality so they can be autoclaved or steam cleaned. It will depend on what country you live in as to the health regulations in each country.

In Australia all tools must be either:-

Single use that you throw away after each use

or

Surgical Steele 315L and highly polished so they can be Autoclaved.

If you do not have an autoclave, you can scrub your tools place them in an autoclave bag , then take them to your local Doctor, Hospital, or Dentist and pay them to autoclave your tools. When they autoclave your tools they must sign your scrubs book, or give you a invoice. The invoice needs to be documented in your scrubs book.

I have explained this later in this manual.

HEMOSTATS

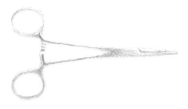

Hemostats are used to hold jewellery and jewellery balls.

FORCEPS

Forceps are used to hold the skin. You can purchase these in a few different shapes and sizes. Pictured below is the Pennington Triangle Forceps, great for a tongue or navel piercing.

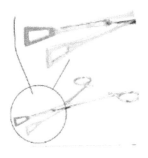

Body Piercing For Students

SPONGE FORCEPS

Sponge forceps can be used for handling dressings and for conducting a piercing. They have a curved mouth and fit into the navel better than a Pennington forceps. I prefer to use the small sponge forceps for the navel and the eye brow piercings.

SLOTTED FORCEPS

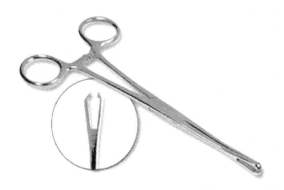

Body Piercing For Students

These are great when you are learning to pierce but they do pinch the client skin more. When you become Professional at piercing you will not need to use them so only buy a small supply?

CALLIPERS

Callipers are used to measure the piercing distance and to measure the gauge of the jewellery. The measuring wheel can be purchased, as a separate tool and I recommend you do buy the calliper and the wheel separately.

Callipers with a Graduated Bowl

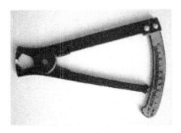

Body Piercing For Students

Vernier Callipers.

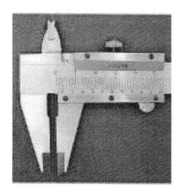

Vernier callipers come in a metal or plastic. Plastic is the best type for measuring the piercing on the skin. It is recommended you use the plastic type for measuring the piercing site. For health reasons you must throw them away after use on each client.

If the jewellery is 10 mm then the dots need to be placed on their skin at 8mm apart. If you place the dots at 10 mm because the jewellery is 10 mm long and then you pierce on the 10 mm dots your will have problems.

The ball will have trouble staying on.

The skin will swell over the ball.

27

Body Piercing For Students

No matter how often the client places ice on the wound/piercing it will still swell a bit.

8mm is $\frac{5}{16}$ inch

10 mm is $\frac{25}{64}$ inch

This is a Calliper and measuring wheel

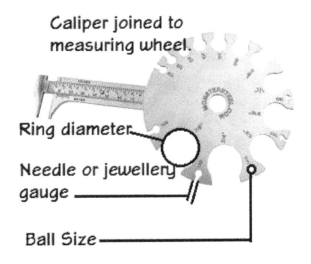

Caliper joined to measuring wheel.

Ring diameter

Needle or jewellery gauge

Ball Size

Although the calliper and measuring wheel is a wonderful tool it is not recommended for the piercing room. However, it is a wonderful tool to have a the sales counter.

Body Piercing For Students

When a customer comes in and needs a ball but does not know the gauge of their jewellery. You can measure the gauge and sell them the appropriate ball size.

SCISSORS

Scissors must be Blunt Sharpe. That means the tips are curved and blunt. The scissors blades must be Sharpe. This is a safe guard so you do not accidently stab the client with a Sharpe point.

These type of scissors can be purchased from your piercing suppliers or from a medical supplier such as Livingston or St. Johns.

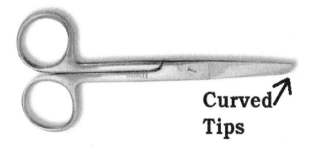

Curved⤴ Tips

BALL HOLDER

A four prong ball holder. These are a great tool. They are not very strong every now and then you need to replace the tool as the prongs break. However, they make life a lot easier to remove and place balls on the jewellery. You are less likely to drop the ball if you use this pronged ball holder to remove from jewellery. When you remove the ball from the jewellery, this tool keeps the screw hole in the correct position ready to place on the jewellery. Got to love that!

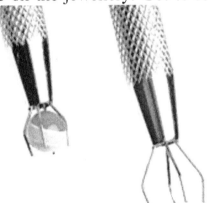

Body Piercing For Students

RUBBER PRACTICE FACES.

Some faces come as a solid rubber face and others need to be placed over foam wig head.

Some have eyebrows and mouths that you replace and you buy them separately.

PORK SKIN

Pig skin, you purchase from your butcher, it is also known as crackling. Pig skin, is an assent while you are practicing, how to mark your piercing distances, your speed and how to become proficient with the handling - of your tools.

Once you feel confident with your tools and speed you can then concentrate on how to perform the entire piercing without moving the bar while you put the jewellery ball in place. Once you learn these things the way to a pain free piercing will start to develop and this is best learned before you start on clients.

When the right amount of tension is on the skins piercing site and the correct speed of the needle insertion has been performed, you now have a hole in the skin. To this point, the client is relieved because you did a professional job and there was little to no pain. Now, this is the part, that many piercers, **get wrong**.

They move the skin as they insert the jewellery and put the ball in place. Once they remove the forceps, they do not pinch each side of the piercing site well enough.

As they insert the jewellery and put the ball in place. The hole is a raw open skin wound and the slightest movement causes the client pain.

Practice over and over how to insert the jewellery and the ball placement, without any skin movement. When you can do this people will spread the word, that you are a professional body piercer.

NEEDLES

Piercing needles come in all gauges. With piercing needles you need to buy one size (gauge) larger than the jewellery size so the jewellery fits inside the hollow needle when you push the needle back out of the skin the jewellery slides into the hole in the skin.

The above photo is the most common type of body piercing needle, a hollow needle features a triangular tip. They come in a variety of gauges as small as 18 gauge and as large as four gauge. The lengths anywhere from 1 1/2 inches to 3 inches. (38.099 mm to 76.199 mm)

Body Piercing For Students

Hollow needles are cut with lasers to ensure sharpness. Jewellery, of the same size as the needle, follows the needle into the piercing hole for insertion. However it is advisable to use a needle of this type one size larger than the jewellery gauge. This way the jewellery fits neatly inside the needle and causes fewer traumas to the flesh and skin cells.

I have seen on some body piercing sites where they discredit this method and advise you to use the same size needle as the jewellery.

As a trainer working with hundreds of students and I have done at least a million piercing over the years, I beg to differ. If the client jumps or flinches as you push the needle through then the jewellery can slip and scratch the skin as the needle makes the hole.

It is not just the skin surface it can scratch, it is the entire skin thickness. Therefore, I strongly recommend you use a needle one size larger than the jewellery. However, I

35

prefer the medical grade needle called a catheter, which I have listed below. When using a catheter with a cannula you use the same gauge as the jewellery.

No one is perfect so we all need to learn safety measures.

The safety measure in this case when using this type of needle use a needle one size larger than the jewellery. This way the jewellery sits inside the hollow needle and glides through the skin.

Do not develop tunnel vision you can always find better ways to do every job. If we could not then we would still need thousands of men to build a house out of stone.

CANNULA /CATHETER NEEDLE

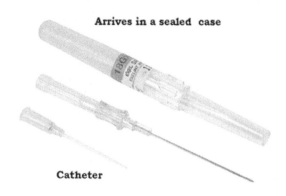

Arrives in a sealed case

Catheter

My favourite way to pierce is with a Cannula / Catheters needle. You buy the same gauge Cannula needle as the jewellery gauge.

The Catheda / catheter stays in the skin after you pierce and you pull the needle out. You insert the jewellery in the cannula (plastic tube) and pull and push the jewellery through the skin hole in one gentle gliding motion. Just like a Surgeon would do. They are also known as, cannula needles. They come in a box of 50 or you can buy as a single item or in packs. In both cases be sure they are in their individual sterile packs.

The jewellery sits inside the cannula (called a hub) while you pull the jewellery through. The hard plastic case around each needle is the throw away that keeps the needle sterilized until you open this sealed pack. The needle has a plastic hub that fits tightly over the needle. When you push through the skin the needle can be pulled out and the hub (the plastic tube called a Catheter/Catheda stays in the skin. The jewellery is placed into the hub, then pulled through the skin.

Providing you keep a firm pinch on the skin this method, does not hurt the person having the piercing. All the skin cells are held in place as you pull the jewellery through.

SHARPS BIN

A Sharps Bin is a must have no matter what size your business is. It is a requirement of the Health And Safety Standards Internationally. Be certain to secure the lid the very moment you place your used needle in the bin.

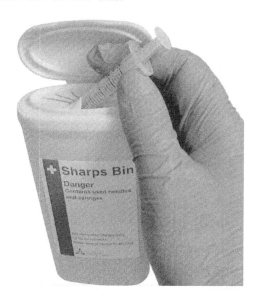

PEDAL BIN

A medical grade pedal bin is both anti-bacterial to help prevent the spread of infection, and heard wearing meaning they can be used again and again without the worry about corrosion or rust. You use your foot to open the bin and your clean-gloved hands never come into contact with the bin. The plastic bag is inserted inside the bin bucket and does not hang outside to the bin.

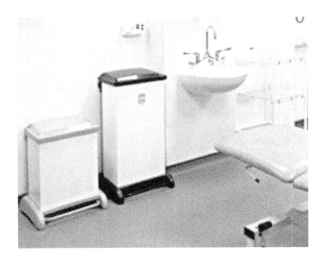

Body Piercing For Students

Body Piercing Tools + Equipment List:-

1. Alcohol 70%
2. Alcohol wipes
3. Aprons plastic
4. Autoclave bags
5. Autoclave or pressure cooker
6. Ball Forceps
7. Ball Pickup Tool
8. Ballinger forceps
9. Bandages
10. Bead Tweezers
11. Betadine
12. Bio hazard sharps container
13. Calipers
14. Clamps/Forceps
15. Corks 1/2 inch
16. Cotton buds
17. Cotton wool pads
18. Cups disposable.
19. Cups shot size
20. Dental Chain
21. Dermal tools
22. Disposable forceps
23. Distilled water
24. Eye loop
36. Jewel measuring wheel
37. Jewellery.
38. Mask
39. Mouth wash
40. Needles
41. Needles-Sleeve-needle.
42. Needles Cathedra
43. Needles Piercing
44. Note pad & pen
45. Paper bed roll
46. Paper towels
47. Pork skin.
48. Povidone-iodine wipes
49. Pressure cooker
50. Q-tip swabs
51. Receiving Tube
52. Ring closing pliers
53. Ring opening pliers
54. Rubber bands
55. Rubber mask.
56. Scissors ... "blunt sharp"
57. Sizing Chart
58. Sharpie marker
59. Steel Wool

41

Body Piercing For Students

25. File (metal)

26. Forceps Ballenger

27. Forceps Forester

28. Forceps Pennington

29. Forceps Septum

30. Gauze pads

31. Gentian violet

32. Gloves latex

33. Gloves Playtex

34. Hemostats

35. Instrument tray

60. Sterilizer bags

61. Tapers

62. Tincture of green soap

63. Tooth brushes soft

64. Tooth picks

65. Tray -Instrument

66. Tray Instrument +lid

67. Trolley

68. Tweezers

69. Tweezers for balls

70. Ultra sonic cleaner

Body Piercing For Students

HOW TO DRESS FOR THE PIERCING ROOM

Sterilization
Includes You
Being Sterile.
This is how you
 grown up for
Proceedures that
draw blood.

Body Piercing For Students

AUTOCLAVE YOUR TOOLS

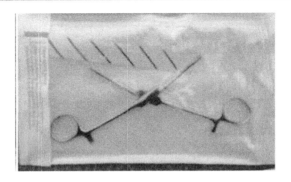

FIGURE 1

When you are autoclaving your tools they must first be scrubbed in a sink that is dedicated to tool scrubbing only. You use green soap a tooth brush and running water to scrub the tools in a dedicated scrubs sink. You must wear gloves. Dry the tools with disposable paper towel.

Then place tool in an autoclave bag in an open position as per this photo. You must use the tag on the bag to date and name the tool and place that tag inside the bag.

The tag will change colour allowing both you and the health department to know that the autoclave sterilizer is working.

Body Piercing For Students

The documentation for the autoclave should be set out in a book like this. The book must be kept next to the autoclave. The " Check by" Columns will be signed by, either someone in your salon or your local Dentist/ Doctor or a hospital staff member. This depends on where the autoclave is.

When sending tools away to be cleaned you need to send the book but keep a photo copy of the book at the salon.

When I first started piercing way back in the 1960s we used a pressure cooker to steam sterilize the equipment. I prefer that method. After the tools were dry we would place them in paper bags.

You could also have a scrubs book and a sterile book. This way one book stays at the salon and the other goes off to the business that is doing your autoclaving for you. Most hospitals do not like you to send the book. They send the items back with a print out of the sterilization details.

STEAM STERILIZATION

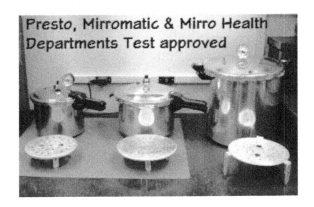

Steaming was used for many centuries to sterilize surgical tools. I myself used a pressure cooker to sterilize my tools for many decades. I love it as I can see the results. They are less expensive than Autoclaves. However, you will need to check with your local health department to ascertain their requirements in your area. You cannot change their mind so it is best to follow what they require and abide by their rules.

Body Piercing For Students

When you have finished scrubbing, your tools with green soap under running water. Place the tools in the pressure cooker. Place the lid on and turn the cooker onto high. Follow the manufacturer instructions.

Tools need to be steamed - for 20 minutes in the pressure cookers and around 2-3

minutes in an autoclave.

STERILIZATION BOOK HEADINGS

Headings for the Sterilization book must include:-

Date

Scrubbed by

Bagged by

Autoclaved by

Time in

Time out

Checked by

Item.

Note; if you are sending them to another facility to be autoclaved you will also need to add another date field next to **TIME IN.**

Body Piercing For Students

Date	Scrubbed By	Bagged By	Autoclaved by	Time In Auto	Time Out	Checked by	Item

When sending tools out to be autoclaved a column for the invoice number must be added.

BODY & FACIAL PIERCING AFTERCARE

Never ever use ointments on an open wound. It will go into the blood system and make you very ill. You may not feel ill for many months, by then you will not know the cause.

Can you imagine this; take out some of your blood mix it with some sticky ointment and inject that blood back into your veins. That is exactly what happens if you put ointment onto an open wound. It mixes with your blood but prevents your blood flowing correctly. I have seen Beauty Therapists put an alcohol rub on their clients when they complete a body wax and I have seen Body Piercers put ointments on the end of their piercing needle before a piercing and Tattooist use a lubricant on their clients. Then sell them an ointment to help the tattoo heal. I have seen mothers loving bath a child's cut and apply ointment to the wound. Ointments were designed for minor surface cuts and abrasions.

NOT OPEN WOUNDS.

Remember, you are being guided here, to follow International Standards.

CLEANING SOLUTIONS

Use either one or all of the following solutions for cleaning the body-piercing site:

1. Packaged sterile saline solution with no additives (read the label!)

Or

2. Non iodized sea salt mixture: Dissolve 1/8 to 1/4 teaspoon of non iodized (iodine free) sea salt into one jug (1 litre) of warm distilled or bottled water. A stronger mixture is not better! Saline solution that is too strong will irritate the piercing. Place the solution into a dark coloured, very clean bottle.

This solution can only be kept for a few days then it must be thrown away and a new batch made.

3. You must first bath the wound in a liquid antimicrobial or germicidal soap lather it up with warm water. Gentle massage the soap into the piercing and rinse off with warm water. Be sure to rinse it extremely well. Then bath with the saline

or the Aromatherapy healer.

4. Aromatherapy Healer. This is a 100% pure and natural healing oil. You buy these from http://www.beautyschoolbooks.com.au or your local Chemist or Aromatherapist.

TEST 1 "**FORMS**"

There are several forms you need to fill in with your client. At this point I would like to point out once you have your diploma / certificate the people you attend to are <u>not</u> your customers they are your clients.

People you sell items too are customers. Clients are people that professionals offer a service too. From the very first day you offer a professional service to someone, they become your client. With this said,

1. Do not ever work on a client in a non professional manor.

2. Be certain that your forms are professional looking.

3. Have your insurance in place before you work on a client.

4. Do not ever use slang.

5. Dress in a professional manor.

6. Be clean and tidy.

7. Have a room dedicated to your professional service.

8. Have your forms numbered.

9. Work to a system.

10. On your client history card have a space to check the number of the forms you have given the client. It is better to be constantly checking what you have done than to tell a client I told you that.

11. When they come back at you and say,

   I have not been told that. You can say but you have signed this form saying I have gone through this with you. You can then show them the signed form and the number of the form that has the information.

When you are new to the industry you may not fully understand the importance of checking systems. Therefore you will need to put your faith in me. Develop good protocols and soon you will be glad you did.

You may have grown up in a family where your grammar was not checked. That is fine we need all types of people to make life interesting and to learn unconditional love. However, you are reading this book because you are smart enough to know you need to improve yourself. The use of slang has to end here today, right now. You are pre-paring to become a professional and professionals do not use slang.

Do not call people honey, love, mate nor any other form of endearment. Use their name.

SUBMIT TEST 1- FORMS

Make all the required forms and send to your teacher to check. First, read all the information you can find in this book and from your peers. Be well informed before setting up your "Forms".

Body Piercing For Students

Naturally as a professional we take nothing for granted. Therefore, we must first seek a clients permission to perform the service or if they are under 18 years of age we need their parent or guardians permission. Some, body piercers and some tattooist will tell you the legal age is 16 but it is not. The legal age is eighteen (18) years of age.

Form 1 Clients permission Form

Salon details go here

Date _____

Name _____

Address: _____
_____PC/Zip _

Phone: _____Mobile_____
I was informed about this service by

_____

I have disclosed all information of known injuries, allergies or any other condition relevant to the treatment I require. I understand that the supplier of the treatments I require must be in full knowledge of any conditions I may suffer in order that the correct treatment be supplied. I acknowledge that the supplier of the treatment I require has taken appropriate measures to ensure the treatment is appropriate and correct. I do not hold the supplier nor the person applying the treatment responsible for any situations resulting from me withholding information.

I hereby release, acquit and forever discharge **Name Of Your Salon Or Service Must Go Here** of all, and from all manner of action and actions, judgements, sums of money and demands whatsoever in law or in equity, which I ever had, now have, or may have against **Name Of Your Salon Or Service Must Go Here** for, upon, or by reason of, any matter or cause whatsoever from the beginning of this day,

Minors Under 18 years of age, must be accompanied, by a parent or guardian or supply a photocopy of the Parents Drivers License or Passport, Signed by the Parent. The Parent must supply two telephone

Body Piercing For Students

numbers and we must be able to contact the Parent on the day of the Piercing to verify their ID.

I do not have Any Heart, Liver, Kidney, Epilepsy Or Allergies/Injuries/Conditions Large Veins or recent Surgery or Implants If yes explain?

_____

Have you ever fainted?

_____

Do you have Aids/ HIV?
Hepatitis?
Diabetes?
Cancer?
Answer

_____

I will not eat for at least two hours before my piercing Yes No
I will not take Aspirin for 8 hours before my piercing Yes No

I give (Salon Name)_____
Technicians Name (_____) To perform my
(Piercing Position Here)_____ piercing.

Body Piercing For Students

Date _____

Client's Signature:_____

Parents ID

_____

Parents Permission Statement / Signature

_____

_____

Parents Work Ph: _____

Home Ph: _____ Mobile_____

Must Be Booked And Paid By

Date_____

Type Of Piercing   _____

Jewellery Size _____

Disclaimer goes here.

Add your salons disclaimer statement here.

FORM 2 - CLIENT HISTORY

As a professional you must keep a client history card in your salon. These cards are private and must not leave the salon or you private computer. However, when you sell the business the client history cards becomes the ownership of the new owner.

Body Piercing For Students

Your Salon Details Go Here			
Name:			
Address:		Tel-Work:	Tel-Home:
Occupation:		D.O.B:	
Medical conditions:		Lifestyle factors:	
		Here you need to know about their sporting activities. If they swim a lot ask them to keep their head above water for a few days and explain they may need more infills than another client	
General health:	Medication:	Known allergies:	
☐ excellent			
☐ good			
☐ poor			

Skin type:	Skin condition:		Notes:	
☐ normal	☐ blemished	☐ coupe rose		
☐ oily	☐ dehydrated	☐ prematurely aged		
☐ dry	☐ sensitive	☐ other		
☐ combination	☐ mature	☐ Eye water a lot		

Previous treatments:	
Body condition:	Postural condition:
Contra-indications:	
Comments / requests:	

TREATMENT	THERAPIST	DATE	PRICE
30 lashes /25 lashes			

Body Piercing For Students

This form must be filled out before the client fills out and signs "Form 1." There are reasons for the Form numbers and I am not going to make this book hundreds of pages explaining all the whys and wherefores. If you do follow my instructions some day you will be glad you did.

In this day and age a Google form may serve your salon well. It can be fill-in online and return automatically to you via email before the client arrives for an appointment.

Body Piercing For Students

Client History Card Form 1

Required

Email address *

your email address

Google Forms
Put salon details
Here

Full Name *

your answer

Address *

your answer

Home Telephone *

your answer

Work Telephone *

your answer

Mobile or Cell Number *

your answer

Date Of Birth *

date
dd/mm/yyyy

Guardians ID Upload Photo ID *

your answer

Guardians Date Of Birth *

date
dd/mm/yyyy

This form can be found on

https://docs.google.com/forms/d/e/1FAIpQ
LSeoyyNhQy3kuK5hYLh5XQCkwmxPod
0jk6VekoyGL1UZg64-
lw/viewform?usp=pp_url

Body Piercing For Students

See if you can improve on this Consultation/ History Card.

"Your Day Spa details go here."

Body Piercing Client History Card

Name:_____ _____
DOB:_____**M / F**

Address:_____
_____ PC_____

Phone: Home _____

 Mobile _____

Email:

_____

Emergency contact name:

_____

Ph: _____
Mob_____

If you are under 18 years of age you must have your Parents/Guardians consent

License Number _____

Parent or Guardians Name:_____

Parent or Guardian Signature:_____

Do you have any of the following?

Aids No ☐ Yes ☐

Hepatitis A B or C No ☐ Yes ☐

High/low blood pressure? No ☐ Yes ☐

If yes, please specify medication_____

–

If you are on blood thinning medication you will not be able to have body piercing without a Doctors Certificate. Do we have

your Doctors certificate
No ☐ Yes ☐

Not applicable No ☐ Yes ☐

<u>Are you any of the following</u>?

Pregnant? No ☐ Yes ☐

Diabetic? No ☐ Yes ☐

Unwell at the moment? No ☐ Yes ☐

On medication? No ☐ Yes ☐

please specify_____

Do you suffer with cold sores? No ☐ Yes ☐

Have you taken any Aspirin or any other drugs today? No ☐ Yes ☐

If Yes Explain

_____

How much alcohol have you had in the last 48 hours? _____Glasses of

_____

65

Body Piercing For Students

Do you faint? No ☐ Yes ☐

Do you have high or Low blood pressure? _____

Do you have any allergies to pigments /anaesthetics? No ☐ Yes ☐

If yes please specify_____

Have you had a Body Piercing previously? No ☐ Yes ☐

If yes any reactions? No ☐ Yes ☐

_____

Lifestyle activities e.g. swimming, gardening etc_____

Do your eyes water very often

No ☐ Yes ☐

If Yes Explain.

_____

Do you suffer from Epileptic fits, fainting, psoriasis, lichen planus,

Darier's disease, acne, eczema,
rosacea, atopic dermatitis, molluscum
contagiosum and active herpes
simplex (cold sore)? Answers

_____

_____

**Are you allergic to any of these
ingredients?**

_____

**What type of drink would the client
like if they are every kept waiting.**

Tea Coffee Black or White

Sugar Sweetener

Prefers water

I have been given Forms.

1_____ 2 _____ 3._____ 4. ___5. _____

Note: Here you must list all the forms
that pertain to the service. The client
must have read the forms and signed to
say they have read the forms. When
they make an appointment I email them

Body Piercing For Students

some of the forms and have them bring
them in. Except Form 2, "The client
history card".

"The client history card" must not leave
the salon.

The client does not need to sign their
history card it is for the salon
information

~~~ *** ~~~

*Note: if you are going to give the client
an anaesthetic you will need to list all
the ingredients. However as a body
piercer that does not have a Diploma in
Beauty you will not be allowed to give a
client an anaesthetic. You can tell them
to buy one at the local Pharmacy
/Chemist and apply it 45 minutes before
they come to your salon for the
piercing. Your insurance does not cover
you for any side effects to anaesthetics.
Do not offer the client a pain killer
either. When I was a wee snip of a girl
we kept Vincent and Bex powders in our
first aid cupboard and if a client had a*

By Robyna Smith-Keys   Page 68

headache we would give them a powder. That cannot happen in this century.

FORM 3 CLIENT APPOINTMENT CARD.

Your business card should be set up in such a way that you can write their appointment program on the card for them. I like cards that fold.

On the front: Put all about you and the salon. Salon name, address, telephone, your name and mobile phone number.

On the inside of the card; have appointment lines with time, date, and service.

On the other inside of the card; have notes to client

On the back of Card; list other services you offer.

A card should be informative and look something like this.

Body Piercing For Students

Front

Middle: On one side have the appointment program. On the other side have lines for notes.

Body Piercing For Students

On the back list your services.

The card will be a normal business card size but will fold like a gift card.

Appointment Program			Notes
Time	Date	For	

It is professional to make an appointment for them to return one week after they have had their piercing so you can check up on their healing process.

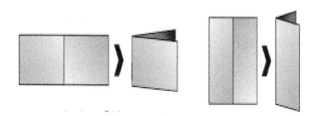

Body Piercing For Students

FORM 4 - CLIENTS TAKE HOME LEAFLET

Body Piercing Students are required to use the following cleaning instructions to make their own personalized take home leaflet for their clients and submit by email to your teacher.

You should start the take home leaflets with your details.

Your name and telephone numbers or Salon name, address and telephone numbers.

Cleaning Instructions

1) WASH your hands with antiseptic soap, thoroughly prior to cleaning, or touching on or near your piercing for any reason.

2) SALINE soak at least two to three times daily. Simply invert a cup of warm saline solution over the area to form a vacuum for a few minutes. The longer you soak the better. For certain placements it may be easier to apply using fresh gauze or a cotton

ball saturated with saline solution. A brief rinse will remove any residue.

3) SOAP no more than once or twice a day. While showering, lather up a pearl size drop of the soap to clean the jewellery and the piercing. Leave the cleanser on the piercing no more than thirty seconds, then rinse thoroughly to remove all traces of the soap from the piercing.

4) DRY with disposable paper products such as gauze or tissues, because cloth towels harbor bacteria and catch on new piercings causing injury. Pat gently to avoid any trauma.

WHAT IS NORMAL? Initially: some bleeding, swelling and tenderness.

During healing: There will be discoloration, itching, and a secretion of a whitish yellow fluid (not pus) that will form a crust on the jewellery. The tissue will tighten around the jewellery as it heals or while swollen.

Ice packs placed on the piercing 4-6 times a day is a must during the 1st few weeks.

73

Body Piercing For Students

While healing: The jewellery may not move freely in the piercing; DO NOT force it.

Cleaning your piercing with a warm saline solution will fix this problem.

Normal but smelly bodily secretions will accumulate and this prevents the jewellery from moving. Your daily hygiene routine will fix this situation.

A piercing may seem healed before healing is actually, complete. This is because piercings heal from the outside in, and although it feels healed the tissue remains fragile on the inside. BE PATIENT, and keep cleaning throughout the entire healing period.

Even healed piercings can shrink or close in minutes after having been there for years! This varies from person to person; if you like your piercing, leave the jewellery in place.

WHAT TO DO. Wash your hands prior to touching the piercing; leave it alone except when cleaning. Always dry with a clean cottonwool pad not your towel. It is not necessary to rotate the jewellery while healing except possibly during cleaning.

Stay healthy. Get enough sleep and eat a nutritious diet. The healthier your lifestyle, the easier it will be for your piercing to heal. Exercise during healing is fine, just "listen" to your body.

Your bedding must be kept clean and changed regularly. Wear clean, comfortable breathable clothing that protects your piercing while sleeping.

Showering is safer than taking a bath, because bathtubs tend to harbour bacteria. If you would like to take a bath, clean the tub well before each use. Then rinse the piercing well with saline after the bath.

DISCLAIMER EXAMPLE.

You will be, well advised to have a solicitor look at your disclaimer. Write out your disclaimer first then the cost will be very small. This is a very important part of your business. The disclaimer must be signed to protect you. I usually make it a separate form and on all of my other forms I have a reference to the Disclaimer such as:-.

I have read and understand the "Disclaimer" yes no . I fully understand the "Disclaimer" Yes No

Disclaimer

Date _____ I _____ Have read all my forms including this Disclaimer I have been given time to read this disclaimer before my treatment.

> ***Note:*** *As soon as you have taken the after treatment photo have the client fill in this section of the disclaimer.*

> I the above named do agree that I have had all aftercare instructions explained to me, I have received a take home sheet and that I fully understand what is required. If I do not follow these instructions I may have healing problems or my procedure may become contaminated.

Body Piercing For Students

. I agree that '*Your salon name here*_____ Day Spa' and its employee's will not be held responsible if my _____ procedure does not heal or becomes contaminated.

Your salon Name here _____ Day Spa has performed my procedure in a clean, hygienic environment as per State Skin Penetrations Act. I have viewed their Local Council License. The tool used were in autoclave bags and the needles were in sealed sterile packs.

No ☐ Yes ☐.

_____ (name of therapist) showed me the setup tray and the sterilized packs before opening them for my procedure. No ☐ Yes ☐

I will return on __/__/20___ for my check up.

Time _____ **Sign:**_____

Body Piercing For Students

Date: _____

Guardian Sign _____
Date: _____

I agreed to the procedure and make note here that I have been informed that this procedure does not carry insurance. I have also been informed of the contra-indications for this procedure. Which may include :-

Now for each service add the contra-indications and possible side effects.

_____

_

Clients Name _____

Signed _____ Dated _____

Witness _____ Date_____

OFFICE USE

WHAT TO AVOID.

Avoid undue trauma such as friction from clothing, excessive motion of the area, playing with the jewellery and vigorous cleaning. These activities can cause the formation of unsightly and uncomfortable scar tissue, migration, prolonged healing, and other complications.

Avoid the use of alcohol, hydrogen peroxide, Betadine, Hibiclens or Ointment during the first week of the healing process.

Avoid over cleaning. This can delay your healing and irritate your piercing.

Avoid all oral contact, rough play, and contact with other peoples bodily fluids on or near the piercing during healing.

Avoid stress and recreational drug use including excessive caffeine, nicotine, and alcohol.

Avoid submerging the piercing in bodies of water such as lakes, pools, Jacuzzis, spas etc.

Body Piercing For Students

Or protect your piercing using a special waterproof bandage which is available from Chemist / Pharmacy / drugstores.

Avoid all beauty and personal care products on or around the piercing including cosmetics, lotions, and sprays, etc.

Don't hang charms or any object from your jewellery until the piercing is fully healed.

~~~~***~~~~

HINTS AND TIPS

Unless there is a problem with the size, style, or material of the initial jewellery, leave it in place for the entire healing period. A qualified piercer should perform any necessary jewellery change that occurs during healing. See APP website for "Picking your Piercer" brochure.

Contact your piercer if your jewellery must be temporarily removed (such as for a medical procedure). There are non-metallic jewellery alternatives.

Leave jewellery in at all times. Even old, well healed, piercings can shrink or close in minutes after having been there for years! If jewellery is removed the reinsertion can be difficult or even impossible. Go to your piercer and have them re-pierce it for you.

With clean hands or soft tissue product, be sure to regularly check the threaded ends on your jewellery for tightness.

("Righty tighty, lefty loosey"). In other words turn to the right to tighten.

Carry a clean spare ball in case of loss or breakage.

Should you decide you no longer want the piercing, seek professional help in the removal of the jewellery and continue cleaning the piercing until the hole closes. In most cases only a small indentation will remain.

For Particular Areas

Navel
To protect the area from restrictive clothing, excess irritation, and impact during physical activities such as contact sports, use a vented eye patch (sold at pharmacies) applied to the piercing under tight clothing (such as nylon stockings and T-Shirts) or secured using a length of ace bandage around the body (to avoid irritation from adhesive). If going for a swim cover completely with a waterproof bandage until it has healed. Sand can travel into the piercing hole.

Body Piercing For Students

Ear/Ear Cartilage and Facial
Use the t-shirt trick: dress your pillow in a large, clean t-shirt and turn it nightly; one clean t-shirt provides four clean surfaces for sleeping.

Maintain cleanliness of telephones, headphones, eyeglasses, helmets, hats and anything that contacts the pierced area.

Use caution when styling your hair and advise your stylist of a new or healing piercing.

Tongue/ Beauty Spot/Labret

Tighten the ball often with clean hands. Rinse your mouth often with a diluted mouth wash. Once it has healed use the mouth wash undiluted. Suck on ice several times a day. Do not smoke or drink alcohol for a few days.

Nipple

The support of a tight cotton shirt or sports bra may provide protection and feel comfortable, especially for sleeping. You may need to keep a clean bandage on the nipple piercing for a week or so. This must be changed twice a day after cleaning the nipple.

Genital

In most cases you can engage in sexual activity as soon as you feel ready. Comfort and hygiene are vital.

During healing all sexual activities must be gentle. To increase comfort and decrease trauma, soak in warm saline solution or plain water to remove any crusty matter, prior to sexual activity.

Use barriers such as condoms, dental dams, and Tegaderm, etc. to avoid contact with a partner's bodily fluids, even in long-term relationships.

Use clean, disposable barriers on sex toys.

Wash hands before touching on or near the piercing.

Use a new container of water based lubricant. Do not use your own saliva as a lubricant.

Body Piercing For Students

After sex, an additional saline soak or clean water rinse is suggested.

Prince Albert piercings can bleed freely for the first few days.

When using medicated soap, please urinate after cleaning the piercing that is near the urethra. Each body is unique and healing times vary considerably. If you have any questions, please contact your piercer.

DISCLAIMER

These guidelines are based on a combination of vast professional experience, common sense, research and extensive clinical practice. This is not to be considered a substitute for medical advice from a doctor. If you suspect an infection, return to your Body Piercer immediately. Do call them first to make a mutually agreed to time. They may suggest you seek medical attention or set up a time for a web-conference with an Aroma-therapist. Keep in mind that the removal of jewellery can lead to further complications. The main complication is the wound hole will close from the outside and pus will not be able to drain away. Be aware that many doctors have not received specific training regarding piercing. Your local piercer may be able to refer you to a piercing friendly medical professional. A Tongue piercing does not carry insurance. As the " International Standards Association" only condone above waist piercings and a tongue piercing is not recommended by the association. If you are having this piercing you do so at your own risk. Balls can come loose while you sleep. Tongue piercings swell and can cause choking. With some people a tongue piercing can cause problems with your speech and harm your teeth. I have read the above and give my permission for the piercing. I do so at my own risk and will not hold the Body Piercing Technician responsible.

Set out your form here like this photo using the below information. As this is a small "Book" I am unable to set it out for you. You may find that if you are working in a salon or studio where they do Tattooing in a

Body Piercing For Students

Country other than Australia Tongue piercings are covered by your insurance company. But, not all insurance businesses know all the rules set by the International Standards Association. If a court case does arise then you might be caught, in a law pursuit you cannot win. Therefore, I suggest you add this Disclaimer to your forms for the piercing positions not covered by the International Standards.

I (Name) _____

Received this form on Date _____

Be sure all these headings are in the client form:-

1. Your check up is date

2. Time

3. Body Piercer Name

4. Your Name

5. Sign

6. Date

Body Piercing For Students

7. A Clients ID Form Should be on the flipside of the disclaimer form

8. Your name address and salon details here

9. Name

10. Address

11. Post code

12. DOB

13. Telephone

14. Parent or Guardians Name On ID

15. ID Type and Number

16. ID Of Client

17. Do you have AIDS Yes No Hep B or C YES No

18. Are you unwell right now

19. Do You Faint Yes No

20. Are You Diabetic Yes No

21. Are You Pregnant Yes No On Medication Yes No

22. How much Alcohol have you had in the last 48 hours

23. Have you taken Aspro or any other drug to day

24. If you give the wrong information it could have a major effect.

25. Date

26. Sign or Guardian Sign

It is imperative to check on the client a week after the piercing. If they do not return for their check up be sure to call them.

27. Ask these questions.

   A. Is your piercing cool to touch?

   B. Has the swelling gone down?

   C. Is there any discharge?

   D. Has the pain subsided?

If they answer "no" to any of these questions and they say they cannot come in for a check up ask them to send you a photo of the piercing straight away and try to offer assistance.

PIERCINGS NOT COVERED BY THE INTERNATIONAL STANDARDS ARE:-

Tongue

Dermal

Genital

Cartilage

With that said, I have noticed that some sites such as safepiercing.org make no reference to the International Standards. Which I found to be, rather curious. I myself sat on the committee that rewrote the Australian Standards for the industry in 1993 and the rewrite of the international standards 2007 to 2014.

~~~***~~~

FORM 4A PIECING AFTERCARE INSTRUCTIONS

Form 4 is what I give them prior to the piercing. Form 4a is the instruction sheet that you give the client after the piercing with a small bag of sea salt attached. You should keep this form brief and to the point.

1. Wash your hands before you touch the piercing and be conscious of the fact that your hands are never ever truly germ free they can cause contamination within seconds.

2. Do not use hydrogen peroxide, alcohol, antibiotic creams, Vaseline, or oil based products on the piercing. Other than Aromatherapy 100 % pure and natural oils.

3. Avoid swimming until healed. The Ocean has sand which could get into your blood. Pools have chlorine, Rivers have mud. However you can use a waterproof bandage.

Body Piercing For Students

4. Never use ointments as this is an open wound and the products can enter the blood system.

5. Do not change the Jewellery until healed.

Cleaning the Piercing

1. Wash your hands with Antibacterial Soap. Put hot water on a cotton wool ball and hold on the piercing. Do this three times. Then put the Aromatherapy Saline Solution on a cotton wool ball and hold onto the piercing.

Do Not Have A Bath During Your Healing Period. When you shower be sure to rinse all soap from the piercing extremely well and use an anti-bacteria soap burning this time.

2. Every night put a 1 teaspoon of sea salt in a cup of boiling water. Allow to cool to bathwater safe temperature and hold the cup on the piercing. It is like you're soaking the piercing. Dry with clean cotton wool.

3. For Oral Piercings Rinse three times daily with Antibacterial, mouthwash. Or

rinse mouth with warm water and sea salt made as above. Grotesque Swelling occurs if you do not Avoid Dairy products, Alcohol, Warm Beverages, Tobacco, Drugs and Hot Spicy Food.

No oral sex or open mouth kissing until mouth is healed. Google Grotesque Swelling.

4. Jewellery I understand that Silver and Gold Jewellery must not be worn until my piercing heals as these metals can leach into the skin and leave a dark stain around piercing.

I (name here)

Of Address

Post Code

Telephone

Mobile

Guardians ID

Guardian to sign

Today's Piercing is

Body Piercing For Students

Dated

I have read and understand the above. I agree that if I do not follow the above instructions I will either get a disease or have healing problems with my piercing. I agree that _____ (*Name of Your Salon Here*) will not be held responsible if my piercing does not heal and becomes contaminated. _____ (*Name of Your Salon Here*) agree to pierce in a professional contaminated free environment thus giving me an attractive clean, hygienic piercing. If they do not treat me in a professional manner and do not use safe piercing practices I will say so immediately. I will fill in the complaints form immediately.

Circle the correct answer.

1. If I forget and touch my piercing without washing my hands what should I do?

Clean my piercing with water. Yes No Wash my hands with soap or antibacterial soap and use warm water or saline solution

or mouth wash to clean the piercing. Yes
No

2. I will clean any discharge with warm
water or Saline or Mouthwash depending
on my Piercers advice. Cotton buds soaked
in Saline and rinse in saline after I have
washed my hands with antibacterial soap.

3. I can go swimming when I get home
today or next week or when my piercing
heals or today as long as I **completely
cover** the piercing with a waterproof
bandage.

4. I can change my Jewellery Tomorrow or
next week or when my piercing heals

4. I can use any kind of Jewellery. Yes No I
can wear silver in three weeks or when my
Piercing Heals or never.

5. I the above have answered these
questions of my own accord. I have crossed
out what does not apply or circled what is
incorrect for my piercing.

I _____ (Name here)

Body Piercing For Students

of (*Salon Name*_____) have checked these answers.

Signature Before piercing _____

Date _____

When piercing is complete & on return for your check up; you are required to fill in this section. The staff have been helpful or very helpful and I feel satisfied that I know how to care for my piercing.

Yes ☐ No ☐

Client's signature after Piercing.

I am completely satisfied with my piercing. It is well positioned and was done in a clean environment with clean and safe materials. I was shown the tools in the satirized bags.

I actually am not happy. Please explain

_____

_____

_____

If the client Name _____

Body Piercing For Students

Is not happy the action plan I have put into place is.

_____

_____

_____

_____

Therapist Name. _____
Signed_____ Dated _____

See attached info.

Sign_____ Dated _____

If we did not take good care of you tell us I am not satisfied.

This is my reason _____

Sign_____ date _____

Your initial check up date is _____

Put this date in there take home pack attached to your card or written on your appointment card. You will be amazed at what you learn about people from that check up visit. If things are not going well they will blame you. This check up appointment helps build a rapport with you client and builds a strong reputation for being a professional.

I once had a young man come back for his tongue piercing to be checked. Within three days his piercing was so badly infected I had to remove his piercing. His breathe sunk and his teeth were slimy. Yet when he come for the piercing his mouth was clean. It was clear he had not cleaned his teeth nor the piercing for three days. His mum a shift worked had not checked on his healing routine.

~~~ * ~~~

We recommend that all Body Piercers do a mini course in Aromatherapy to assist their clients with aftercare. Note; If you are a Professional Body Piercer under the Beauty Therapy Insurance Guidelines they do not cover Tongue, Genital or Skin Anker piercings. Therefore, if you are offering Tongue or Genital or skin Anker piercings you need to make your client aware that there is no insurance for these piercings should anything go wrong. They have this piercing at their own risk. Anker piercings cause permanent damage to the skin and can only be repaired with plastic surgery.

Tongue piercings do cause problems with teeth, speech and balls may come loose and cause choking Also there is a danger of the ball coming off during sleep and getting stuck in the air pipe and causing death. A tongue piercing can also cause problems with speech. Otherwise you need to find an insurance company that does cover Body Piercing of those parts. Now complete test 1 and submit to your teacher.

Note to student

It is a good idea to turn the aftercare and the disclaimer into a small booklet. Place a small bag of deep sea salt inside with your business card. Add a small explanation on how to care for their piercing with the salt. Not everyone will be able to buy the aftercare you have on offer.

Body Piercing For Students

I have written an entire book on ear piercings. I trust this information will be sufficient until you read the ear piercing book which also covers the entire do's and don'ts on piercing with a gun.

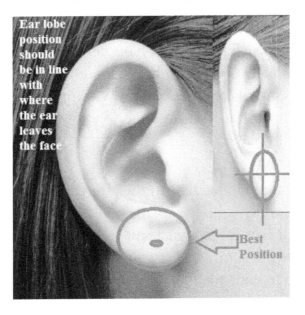

Ear lobe position should be in line with where the ear leaves the face

Best Position

Ear piercing is an almost universal practice for men and women. At various times in history, men wore elaborate earrings; during the Elizabethan era many famous men such as Shakespeare, Sir Walter Raleigh and Francis Drake wore gold rings in their ears.

"As the Roman Republic grew more effeminate with wealth and luxury, earrings were more popular among men than women; no less a he-man than Julius Caesar brought back to repute and fashion the use of rings in the ears of men.

PLACEMENT OF EAR PIERCINGS

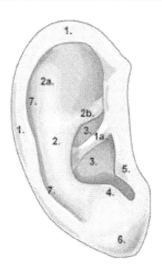

1. Helix

2. Antihelix -- with two subparts:

2a: the superior crux

2b: the inferior crux

3. Concha called couch by us

4. Antitragus

5. Tragus

6. The lobe

7. Scapha

There are thirteen names for ear piercing positions and about 25 actual positions. Please remember this: you are training to become a Professional Body Piercing Technician. The more you learn the more Professional you become. The more Professional you are the more you will realize that piercing through ear cartilage boarders on brutality. Positions such as the

2: Antihelix

2a: the superior crux

2b: the inferior crux

Scapha piercings are very painful to have pierced and seldom heal completely. Making money can be the "Root Of All Evil" or an absolute joy. Pharmacy assistants can learn to pierce ears with a gun in one hour. They feel they are trained in Professional Ear Piercing. They are even given a certificate to say they are professionals. I am not condemning their ignorance I am simply advising you to develop your integrity.

Do you know where the Scapha piercing is? Your teacher will ask you about this piercing name and you will have researched it and should be able to answer her questions. So do your homework now.

When you pierce an earlobe with a needle the hole is hollow and clean.

When you pierce with a gun the needle is solid so it does not remove a piece of skin and flesh. It is like a bullet wound it scatters the flesh. I am aware that to have a piercing done with a gun is very inexpensive and that's the main attraction. But become educated enough to advise your clients against it without condemning it. It is better that you offer gun piercings then a Hairdresser or Pharmacy assistant that has no understanding of the healing complications. As a professional you need to give your client informed options and information.

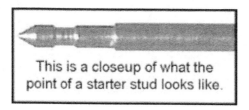

This is a closeup of what the point of a starter stud looks like.

If a mother of four or five girls all want their ears pierced it is more beneficial to her to pay a $100 for them all to have their ears pierced in comparison to $125 or more each. She can buy a lot of food with that extra money. So do not make her feel bad. Give her a big discount to have their ears pierced with the needle. Even if a single parent or low income family can save $10 it's a massive help to them. You may have to pierce the earlobes of a large family with the gun.

So come down to earth and learn both methods.

Forget all the nonsense about guns being unhygienic. The stud earring is in a sterile container. The stud pierces the ear not the gun and the gun does not touch the ears.

You might even learn all there is to learn about gun piercings. Invest the money in the gun and stock and never use it if you know how to nurture people correctly. That is what it takes to become a professional. That's what it takes to be the best in the business.

Give clients the option to choose after you have informed them of the difference. Do not give that information in such a way they feel uncomfortable about choosing the gun for ear lobe piercings.

Never ever pierce other parts of the body with a gun.

Only ever pierce the lobe with a gun after giving the client all the necessary information. The finale choice has to be theirs.

The next photo is a hole made with a piercing gun when looked at with a microscope. There is far more trauma done to the hole in the skin with a gun than with a needle.

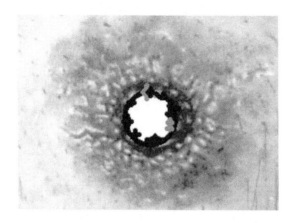

When you pierce an earlobe with a needle the hole is hollow and clean.

However, if you the piercer, performs the insertion and the removal of the needle in a jagged movement, they will add trauma to the skin.

How still you keep the jewellery while putting the ball in place and how well you pinch the skin until the process is completed, is of vital importance.

Body Piercing For Students

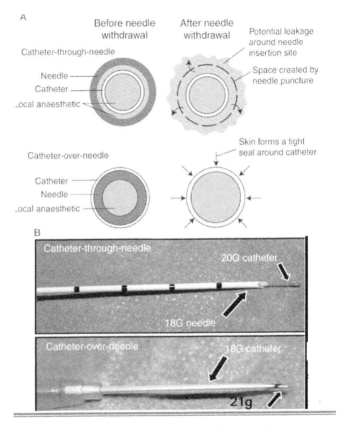

The hole made with a cannula needle can also be traumatized should you move the piercing site while placing the ball on the jewellery.

EAR SEEDLING

Ear seeds stimulate those points naturally and non-invasively.

Many are unfamiliar with this practice, which utilizes acupressure rather than acupuncture. Small metal beads, or vaccaria seeds, are pressed into the corresponding pressure points, and a piece of adhesive tape is applied over so that they are held in place. This allows the wearer to receive continuous benefits for days at a time, and you can even press on the bead to reactivate it during this time.

Often described as reflexology for the ear, there are hundreds of points on the ear that are believed to represent a micro-system of the whole body, with points for areas both physical and emotional.

Ear Seeding Chart

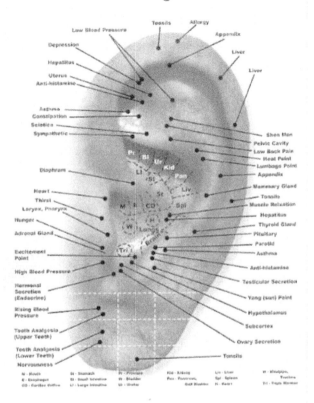

The stimulation of these points is known as Auriculotherapy. You could also study acupressure as an added service to body piercing.

EAR PIERCING AND ACUPUNCTURE POINTS

I would advise you to get an ear acupuncture or acupressure chart and when piercing the ears aim for a healing position.

As a novice at acupuncture, do not advise your client. Always say I am not trained in acupuncture nor acupressure but I am lead to believe that :-

example: The piercing of (and name the point) is known to relieve (name the ailment)

EAR CARTILAGE

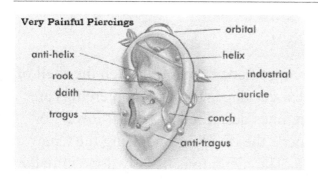

Very Painful Piercings

anti-helix
rook
daith
tragus

orbital
helix
industrial
auricle
conch
anti-tragus

Body Piercing For Students

It is important to explain that these cartilage piercings seldom heal completely and leave permanent scars. Furthermore, they continue to hinder sleep patterns.

ANTITRAGUS:

A piercing is made through the extrusive ridge of cartilage opposite the tragus. In most cases, a straight or curved barbell is advisable over a ring.

BRIDGE: INDUSTRIAL, LADDER:

 A barbell pierced through the two sides of the upper pinna so that it looks like a bridge.

CONCH:

Piercings made straight through the shell of the ear cartilage. The Conch piercings are sometimes described as either "lower" or "upper", the dividing line being the Crus helix. The piercing is usually done initially with a barbell, but once it's healed a large ball-closure ring may be inserted, spiked

Body Piercing For Students

labret studs, are sometimes worn as well. However, spikes are not- recommended for new piercings.

DAITH:

A piercing made through the Crus helix, the innermost ridge of cartilage above the Tragus. Of the interior ear cartilage piercing, the Daith usually heals the most successful as it is not subject to pressure from sleeping and irritation from daily activities.

HELIX:

Piercings made through or around the upper, curled edge of the ear, including the curled edge towards the face. If the curl is extreme or wide, a piercing made parallel to the plane of the head through the apex of the curl will be more comfortable. In this instance, a piercing made perpendicular to the plane of the head would require a large diameter ring to allow for proper healing which would be too large to comfortably fit between the ear and head.

113

LOBE:

The most common piercing of the ear can be pierced several times depending on its size. One of the fastest of all piercings to heal.

ORBITAL:

A ring through the upper conch so that the ring comes out either side.

ROOK:

A piercing made through the antihelix, the ridge above the "Daith" ridge. More prone to rejection/migration.

SNUG:

A horizontal piercing of the antihelix, across from the tragus. This piercing isn't suitable for all people.

Body Piercing For Students

TOP-EAR "PINNA":

The outer rim of the ear extending from the top of the Helix to the Daith. The second most common piercing, it has become quite popular because it's novel without being too extreme. Usually takes 12 months to heal and is more prone to Granulomas because of hair pulling on it and lying on it during sleep.

TRAGUS:

The prominence of cartilage, in front of the opening of the ear canal. This piercing is a little bit more painful than other cartilage piercings because it's very thick, usually takes at least 12 months to heal.

This is an ideal piercing for people that suffer from migraine. It stimulates the adrenal gland and assists with fatigue by energizing the client. It has been proven to work on 89% of migraine sufferers. This is also a good point to prevent hunger.

Body Piercing For Students

TRANSVERSE:

A horizontal piercing pierced through the lobe. Usually pierced with a barbell.

EAR JEWELLERY

Ear piercing studs aren't really suitable for initial piercing because they can't be cleaned properly which can lead to infections. Sleepers are also unsuitable because they have tiny sharp hinges that tear the inside of the piercing causing inflammation and delaying healing.

Most body piercers, use ball closure rings (a ring with a ball in it) because they don't come out and have no sharp edges. The only metals, which should be used for the healing period, are 18ct Gold, Niobium, Titanium, Surgical Stainless Steel or a hypoallergenic plastic. However, the ball closer rings can also be difficult to learn how to close without disturbing the pierced site. I prefer above all, the horseshoe shaped jewellery for the new piercing.

Body Piercing For Students

It is very easy to put one ball on the end of the jewellery without disturbing the piercing site and easy for the client to clean. These come in open hoops and Circular Barbells.

CIRCULAR BARBELLS

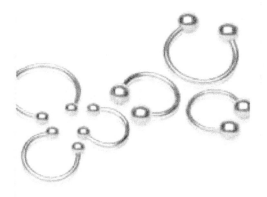

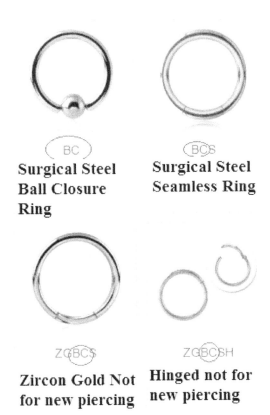

BC

Surgical Steel Ball Closure Ring

BCS

Surgical Steel Seamless Ring

ZGBCS

Zircon Gold Not for new piercing

ZGBCSH

Hinged not for new piercing

HORSESHOE HOOPS

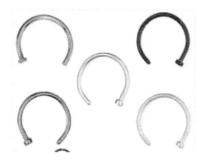

EAR HEALING

The ear lobe is one of the fastest parts of the body to heal. It usually takes 6-10 weeks to heal and problems are very rare. Cartilage piercings however, take longer to heal and are more prone to problems. This is because cartilage doesn't have the same cells that from scar tissue as flesh. The most common problem is small lumps that form around the piercing; these are called Granulomas and usually occur because the piercing has been knocked or the Jewellery has been taken out and re-inserted damaging the wound.

Body Piercing For Students

The best course of action to heal Granulomas is to apply hot compresses to the wound once or twice a day. Put a clean paper towel under hot tap water, make sure that it's not hot enough to burn the skin, but hot enough to penetrate the wound. Leave on till the heat dissipates, do this twice a day. If that doesn't work the best course of action is to remove the Jewellery for a short period of time to allow the wound to heal. When the lump goes down (usually 4-5 days) the jewellery may be reinserted, however, if the lump reoccurs, it's best to let it heal and have it re-pierced at a later date.

Another problem is "Keloids". They are lumps that come from excessive scar tissue formation, this problem is genetic and people with black or dark skin are especially prone to it. If a Keloid develops it's best to remove the jewellery as they can be very hard to treat, the best treatment is the application of "Cortisone" cream that you must get on prescription from a physician. It has been noted that keloid tend to form more often around the exit hole,

Body Piercing For Students

due to the action of the needle, which slices
a crescent-shaped opening.

EAR AFTERCARE PRODUCTS

You will need to purchase the following
products from a chemist or the supermarket.

Don't use Hydrogen peroxide, Betadine,
Methylates Spirits, alcohol swabs, or
alcohol-based cleansers on the piercing, as
they are very astringent and destroy the
cells, which form scar tissue. Don't use
creams or ointments as they keep the
wound moist, when it needs to be dry and
this hampers the healing process.

Triclosan based antibacterial
solutions – Physohex or Sapoderm.

Lavender Oil – make sure it's the
"Essential Oil" of lavender or has
(BP) to ensure it is medicinal grade.
Never use it neat always mix it with
base oil.

Sea Salt. To make salty water
solution. (Don't use table salt as it

contains Iodine which hampers wound healing).

Gauzes, paper towel or tissue to use for hot compresses.

B Vitamins with Zinc to promote healing. (Optional)

Body Piercing For Students

EAR JEWELLERY OPTIONS

Explain their jewellery options.

After your piercing is healed you can wear a variety of commercially available earrings, however, you should avoid silver as it oxidizes and can cause allergic reactions and Argyria (a permanent black mark in the wound). We have rings in Steel, titanium, niobium, 22ct gold hard plated steel, 14ct dental alloy and 9 - 18ct gold.

DO'S & DON'TS -EAR PIERCING

The Number One Cause Of Infection Is Touching And Playing With The Piercing, Only Touch It When Cleaning!

DO use a Triclosan based anti-bacterial soap (Physohex or Sapoderm, available at any chemist or supermarket) to clean the piercing in the shower (once a day only!).

Soak the piercing under the shower for 1-2 minutes, then put 1-2 drops (no more!) of the cleaning solution in your hand, lather it up and apply the lather gently to the piercing. Leave the lather on for 1 minute, then soak the piercing once again and wash thoroughly to remove all the solution.

Leaving the solution on your skin can cause irritation! Neglecting to use anti-bacterial soap for the full healing period may result in infection.

DO dissolve quarter a teaspoon of sea-salt in a cup of boiling water. Let this cool a little to the temperature of a hot bath, then soak a clean gauze or piece of paper towel in the solution, apply this to the piercing for 2-3 minutes.

You can also use Saline solution (available at any chemist) although it's not as effective because it's cold. Rinse afterwards with fresh water and dry thoroughly with a clean tissue or piece of toilet paper. Not drying the area afterwards promotes the growth of bacteria and increases the chance of infection. Hot salty water irrigation of the wound is the best way to promote healing.

DO use Lavender oil as it promotes healing and lubricates the wound reducing tenderness. Apply a small amount with a cotton-wool bud after cleaning then move the jewellery gently so it gets into the wound. Remove any excess with a tissue as leaving it on can cause the skin to become irritated. It may be purchased at supermarkets (medicine section) or at chemists and must be marked (BP) or medicinal grade.

DO check the piercing every morning to ensure that your hair hasn't become entangled in the jewellery. If you have long hair it's advisable to use a bobby pin to keep your hair of the piercing until it's healed. With Top-ear piercings it's advisable to get your hair cut a little shorter to keep it of the piercing as the hair aggravates the piercing and increases the likelihood of infection.

DO be careful when brushing your hair not to catch the jewellery in the brush as this can tear the wound and cause inflammation.

DO make sure that you use clean pillowcases and bedding to reduce the likelihood of microorganisms getting into the wound.

DON'T turn the ring in the wound for the first 2-3 weeks as this aggravates the wound, after that you may turn the ring gently once it's been cleaned to allow the lavender oil to penetrate the wound.

DON'T remove the jewellery during the healing phase; putting it in and out can increase the likelihood of infection. Leaving the jewellery out during the healing phase can lead to the hole closing up.

DON'T replace the jewellery with sleepers as they have tiny sharp hinges that aggravate the piercing and cause inflammation. Silver sleepers are especially dangerous as the silver oxidizes in the wound and can lead "Argyria" a permanent black mark in the skin.

DON'T put the headpiece of the phone on the ear that's pierced; be especially careful of this with public phones. If both ears are pierced make sure to clean the earpiece of the phone with disinfectant.

DON'T get hairspray or cosmetics on the piercing during the healing phase. When washing your hair make sure to wash the piercing carefully.

Body piercers Note; when positioning for an earlobe piercing be sure to centre the mark inside a visual circle.

Body Piercing For Students

TEST 2
TRAY SETUPS BODY PIERCING

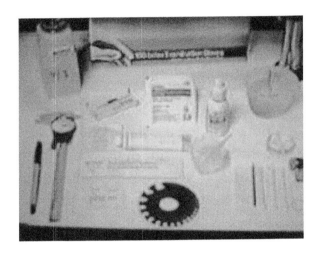

This photo is what a piercing tray should look like when ready for you to do a piercing. However, if you are using a cannula / catheter needle you will also need sterile scissors.

Although this student is very neat, some main tools are missing from this setup.

They are forceps, ball holder, hemostats, ice, gauze, and camera. For a mouth piercing the missing items would be, spit cups, dental chain and paper towel plus mouthwash. Plus they did not have disposable calipers on their tray.

1. Read all the below information for all piercing.

2. Add any information to each set up and procedure that has been left out.

3. Set up A4 sized laminated sheets. On each sheet name the piercing position and everything that needs to go onto a piercing tray for that piercing.

4. On the flipside put the piercing procedure.

5. . Be sure you know how to prepare your client. Bibs on for mouth piercings, before the cleaning process, of the piercing site. Gauze around ears. Head bands on for all facial piercings or use a paper cap.

Body Piercing For Students

Put gauze around ear. Then place the head band or the cap.

Note on some of the tray Setups in the following pages we may have left something out. See if you can find what is missing type it in and highlight it in red. Submit each page for each piercing to your teacher via email first before you have the pages laminated.

Remember this needs to be set out in such a way that if you are having an off day you can look at this sheet to check your tray before you begin the piercing.

If something you need is missing or not in a ready state then you may have to try to hold the piercing while you reach somewhere else for the item. This would seem very unprofessional to your client. Remember they are nervous.

Watch DVDs several times before trying to do this test.

The tray setups in this book are for Australian methods (Catheda Needle) of piercing not the USA method.

HINTS

It is wise to raise their arms above their head straight after you have placed the ball on the piercing. This slows down the bleeding.

It is wise to set up the tray while they fill in the forms and read and sign the disclaimer. It is best if you have everything ready for them when they enter the room. This way you can make light conversation to ease their mind.

Body Piercing For Students

It is wise to take their pulse when you have completed the piercing or take their blood pressure.

They may look and say they feel fine when you have finished the piercing but in fact may be light headed and will not realize this until they get up to walk away.

It is important to give them an ice block or a glass of cold water before they leave. Be sure to check that you add this to your procedures list. OR YOU WILL LOOSE MARKS.

LABRETS AND BEAUTY SPOTS

Best labret Jewellery is 14 gauge Labret Barbell 10 mm in length. They come in screw in and ball screw on. For a new

piercing use the large pain un-jeweled ball in surgical steel or PTFE bar with surgical steel ball.

Beauty Spot use 10 mm length 16 gauge plain 5 mm surgical steel ball.

BEAUTY SPOT

Jewellery Selection "Labret Barbell"

Gauge 16

10 or 12 mm in length

Ball 5 or 6 mm diameter

Surgical stainless steel labret barbell is initially required, depending on the thickness of the client's lip. In the case of collagen lips, a 12 mm stem is required. If the barbell is too tight, the skin inside the mouth will begin to grow over the back of the barbell and will become embedded in the lip, so it is best to start with a larger stemmed barbell and then downsize when the swelling subsides to a 6 mm — 8 mm

Body Piercing For Students

IV Cannula Needle — 16 gauge

Jewellery Labret 16 gauge 10 or 12 mm long.

2 cups of Listerine. Dilute the mouth wash with half water

2 Spit cups

Marker Pen Shapie

2 Cotton Wool Pads

Ice Pack

2 gauze pad one that is cold sitting on Ice.

Forceps

Hemostats

Scissors

Alcohol wipe

Betadine

Dental Chain

Body Piercing For Students

Paper towel.

2 squares of gauze.

Camera

Be sure to remove the ball with Hemostats prior to the piercing. All jewellery must be autoclaved. Be sure the jewellery has air dried before placing it in the Cannula. A Cannula is the plastic tube which covers the needle.

Be sure to open the sterile needle in front of the client not before they enter the room.

Check for nicks in the cannula.

Have your tray very close to you.

PROCEDURE BEAUTY SPOT

Prepare client

Put paper towel with dental chain aroud their neck

Get the client to rinse with diluted Listerine (mouth wash)

Client can be semi reclined.

Placement of the piercing site is usually in line with the incisor about 1 cm above the top lip. Do this with a small dot made with the sharpie (pen). Get client's opinion and go ahead as to the placement.

Now take a photo and ask the client to sign the position approval form.

Spray Xylocaue inside the lip. But, if you do spray with Xylocaue the client must stay for six hours.

WHY? So you can check they do not bite their tongue, you must check on them every 5 minutes. They must hold their tongue with a clamp during this time. My

137

recommendation is do not use the Xylocaue. A good Body Piercer knows how to pierce painlessly.

Go in wide with the clamp not to drag on the skin / flesh. Place the forceps/clamps over the lip and pull out.

Have the clients keep their teeth together throughout the procedure. This is an absolute must.

Keep an eye on them to be sure their teeth are together at all times. If they keep their teeth together, this will prevent them swallowing the ball, should it drop into their mouth as you place the ball on the jewellery stem.

Some clients will grab your piercing hand as you pierce therefore, I always ask them to sit on their hand.

Coming from the outside of the lip proceed to pierce through the skin. Ensure the plastic taper is protruding inside the lip and discard the needle.

Body Piercing For Students

Cut the cannula both ends. Be sure to keep the forceps firm and that they have their teeth together before you cut and while you cut.

Now pinch the skin very firmly alongside the cannula with cotton gauze wrapped around your fingers as their mouth is slippery hold tight and remove the forceps.

Insert the jewellery from the inside of the mouth and feed through, removing the cannula at the same time.

 Hold the barbell firmly in place with finger while removing the cannula so it sticks out well, remove the cannula and secure bead onto barbell.

Do not release the pinch until the ball is in place.

Rinse their mouth and hold a spit cup firmly against their lower lips and tell them to spit. Wipe their mouth with a paper towel.

Beauty spots usually swell up more than labret piercings. Suggest that the Client

Body Piercing For Students

sucks on ice to reduce swelling. I supply them with a lemonade iceblock.

But there is something's that are missing from this procedure and the tray set up.

After you read my best tip and hints add to the above tray set up and this procedure, the missing information.

This procedure should be on the back of the tray set up sheet.

Now here is the best tip I can give you.

The skin has many thousands of cells that you are moving. They go inside the needle that is what we call a puncture. The firmer you hold the forceps without bruising the skin the less painful the piercing. The faster you puncture the skin the better. If you can manage to do those two things correctly the client will be amazed at how little it hurts. But there is more

If you take off the forceps now and insert the jewellery, remove the cannula and screw on the ball.

The pain will be unbearable.

The piercing puncture swells immediately and Mother Nature is trying to fill in the hole and thousands of cells are rushing to the wound to heal it and close up the hole.

DO NOT EVEN FOR A SPLIT SECOND release the pressure on the site of your pinch, until you have completed the piercing, inserted the jewellery and put on the ball.

 The very instant you put on the ball, add a cool wet cloth and add pressure to the site.

Then and only then you may release your fingers that are pinching the site.

The cold wet gauge should have come out of a freezer just moments before you do the piercing and be sitting on an ice block. Practice this method on your training mask and pork skin. Your teacher will be showing you this over a Web-Conference and on your practical training day.

Body Piercing For Students

EYE BROW

Special' Considerations

Eyebrow piercing is one of the more dangerous piercings.

So it is a good idea to use a bright light and magnifying glasses to check where their veins are located. I usually use a curved barbell 16 gauge. I place the Barbell on the face and tape it and ask them to look sideways.

Be sure the lower ball sits above the Frontal bone edge otherwise there will be bruising should the client lie on their face.

Jewellery Selection

Straight Bar Bell or CBR or CBR
Gauge 16 or 14
Length 10-14 mm

TRAY SET UP EYEBROW

1. Needle IV cannula 16 or 14 gauge depending on the size of your client but the norm is 16 gauge.

2. Appropriate jewellery CBR or Curved Barbell

3. Clamps/Forceps

4. Sharpie/marking pen

5. Hemostats

6. Scissors

7. Cotton wool pads

8. Betadine diluted in a small cup

9. Alcohol wipes

10. Iced gauze sitting on ice pack.

11. Touch.

12. Callipers

13. Head band or cap

Body Piercing For Students

14. Camera

PROCEDURE EYEBROW

1. First Attend to client, fill in forms and lay the client down. Put paper towel under their head and over their shoulders. Use a torch to look for the veins.

2. Use alcohol swab and clean area.

3. Check for veins with a torch and wear your magnifying head set.

4. Apply proviodine iodine to area known as Betadine

5. With your fingers pinch along the are you are considering to place the piercing. The client has little to no reaction when you do not pinch a nerve. However, when you pinch a nerve they feel a different sensation. If is vitally important not to pierce a nerve.

6. Have client sitting up when placing the marks on the Eyebrow. Use callipers and place marks on either side of the eyebrow 8 mm apart for 10 mm jewellery 10 mm apart for 12 mm jewellery.

7. Lie client down and stand behind their head.

8. Apply clamps to the skin so the piercing points are visible.

9. Proceed to pierce through the Eyebrow from the underside, ensuring the cannula is protruding at least 2 mm in behind the exit hole.

10. Cut the cannula.

11. Pinch the skin firm around the cannula.

12. Take off the forceps

13. Insert Jewellery into cannula and feed the jewellery through from the outside, removing the cannula at the same time. Keep a firm grip on the

piercing site with one hand and place the ball on the jewellery. This is like your fingers are forceps. The pinch must keep the site firm and stop the jewellery from moving while you screw the threaded ball onto the barbell. Ensure that the ball is securely tightened and in place.

14. To reduce bleeding have them put their hands above their head for a few minutes.

15. Place gauze and an ice pack on the site. Apply pressure to the piercing site with the ice cold pad.

16. Clean the piercing site.

17. Take their pulse and be certain they are feeling normal before you allow them to get off the bed.

18. Take photo and be certain they are happy with the piercing and have them confirm so, in your forms.

Body Piercing For Students

If using captive bead. Check that the bleeding has subsided before you continue to place the bead into the ring.

TEST 3

What is wrong with the eyebrow procedure?

Rewrite the procedure and submit as

 "Test 3 of exam 7, small book."

LABRET TRAY SETUP

Jewellery Selection

Labret Barbell

Gauge 14

Length 10 to 14 mm

Ball diameter should be 6 mm for a new piercing. It will be less painful when they tighten the ball every night before they go to bed.

147

Body Piercing For Students

Surgical stainless steel labret barbell is initially required, depending on the thickness of the client's lip. In the case of collagen lips, a 12 mm stem is required.

If the barbell is too tight, the skin inside the mouth will begin to grow over the back of the barbell and will become embedded in the lip, so it is best to start with a larger stemmed barbell and then downsize when the swelling subsides to a 6 mm — 8 mm

You will need to charge extra but for the Labret, Tongue and Beauty spot offer PTFE jewellery.

TRAY SET UP

LABRET / MUNROE / BEAUTY SPOT

1. Listerine/ Dilute the mouth wash with half water in a cup.

2. A spit cup

3. Cup for jewellery.

4. Sharpie. Marker Pen

5. Callipers

6. Cotton Wool Pads

7. Sterile single use IV cannula — appropriate for jewellery which is 14 gauge

8. Appropriate jewellery — labret barbell

9. Clamps/forceps

10. Hemostats

11. Scissors

12. Dental chain and paper towel

13. Alcohol wipes

14. Gauze

15. Ice pack

16. Camera

PROCEDURE LABRET / MUNROE / BEAUTY SPOT

Body Piercing For Students

1. Attend to client. Check that all forms have be filled in.

2. Get the client to rinse with diluted Listerine.

3. Place the Jewellery in a small cup of Betadine. Be sure to remove the ball with Hemostats prior to the piercing.

4. Client can be semi reclined

5. Placement of the piercing site is usually in line with the incisor about 1cm below the bottom lip. Get client's opinion and go ahead as to the placement.

6. Take a photo of the placement dots after the client confirms they are happy with the placement.

7. They must sign the form to say they are happy with the placement.

8. Spray Xylocaine inside the lip. But if you do the client must stay for 12 hours

9.   WHY so you can check they do not bit their tongue you must check on them every 5 minutes. They must hold their tongue with a clamp during this time. My recommendation is do not use the Xylocaue. A good Body Piercer knows how to Pierce painlessly.

10. Place the clamps over the lip and pull out. Go in wide with the clamp not to drag on the skin / flesh

11.Have the clients keep their teeth together throughout the procedure.

12.Coming from the outside of the lip proceed to pierce through the skin. Ensure the plastic taper is protruding inside the lip and discard the needle.

13. Cut the top of the cannula

14. Be sure you have a tight grip with a cotton pad of the skin and flesh around the cannula before you take away the forceps.

15.Insert the jewellery from the inside of the mouth and feed through, removing the cannula at the same time. Hold the barbell firmly in place with finger while removing the cannula so it sticks out well, remove the cannula and secure bead onto barbell.

16. Rinse their mouth and hold a spit cup firmly against their lower lips. Tell them to spit. Wipe their mouth with a paper towel.

17.Suggest, have the client suck on ice to reduce swelling. I supply them with a lemonade ice bock. Providing they are not allergic to any of the ingredients and they do not have sugar diabetes.

18.Ask then to put their hands above their head. While their hands are above their head, keep ice and pressure on the piercing site.

19. Take their Pulse.

20. Have them approve the piercing and sign the form again.

21. Take a photo.

NIPPLE

Special' Considerations:

Nipples come in all sizes, so it is imperative that you choose the correct jewellery for your client. Some men have extremely small nipples, so the piercing sometimes has to go through the areola and this must be discussed with your client to make sure

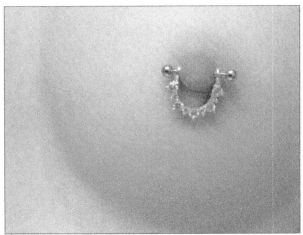

they don't mind. I advise women that with all piercings there is scarring, so the piercing of the nipple may or may not cause a problem with breast feeding. Leave it to her to decide.

In this picture the piercing was placed at the base of the areola, this is an excellent position.

Nipple piercing is one of the more painful piercings, so it is a good idea to offer some numbing cream beforehand (*emla cream patch*). This must be applied one hour prior to the piercing. Ensure you cover the Emla cream well so as not to expose it to the air. Emla patches are ideal for this. Suggest the client purchase her own and apply 40 minutes before her appointment time.

NIPPLE JEWELLERY SELECTION

Straight or curved barbell (Best choice is a curved barbell.)

Gauge 14 always use 14 g

Length 10-14 mm

Body Piercing For Students

Nipple Tray Set up

1. Needle IV Cannula 14g

2. Appropriate Jewellery CBR or Barbell

3. Clamps/Forceps

4. Hemostats

5. Scissors

6. Alcohol wipe

7. Betadine in cup

8. Sharpie

9. Callipers

10. Cotton pads

11. Gauze

12. Bandages

13. Ice. Place gauze on ice pad

14. Camera

PROCEDURE FOR NIPPLE

1. Use alcohol swab and clean area.

3. If the nipple in inverted you will need to place ice on the nipple and gently pinch until it pops out.

2. Apply proviodine iodine to area or Betadine

3. Have client sitting up when placing the marks on each side of the nipple. Place marks on either side and at the base of the nipple.

Take a photo after they approve the position and sign the approval form.

4. Lie client down in a semi reclined position..

5. Apply clamps to the skin so the piercing points are visible.

6. Proceed to pierce through the nipple from the outside, ensuring the needle is

protruding at least 1 cm in front of the exit hole. Pinch each side of the cannula and remove the forceps.

7. Insert Jewellery into cannula, removing the cannula at the same time.

8. Apply pressure to the piercing site with wet cold cotton gauze.

9. Check that the bleeding has subsided and continue to place the bead into the ring or screw the threaded ball onto the barbell. Ensure that the ball is securely tightened and in place. Clean the piercing site.

Ask then to put their hands above their head. While their hands are above their head keep ice and pressure on the piercing site.

Take a photo.

Cover with Bandage.

Take their Pulse.

Have then sign the forms.

Body Piercing For Students

Special Considerations

The oral cavity is well known for its rapid healing properties due to its ability to form a Lining which is called a lingual protein. For example, after drinking a hot cup of tea/coffee and losing the lining from the roof of your mouth, within a few hours this area will heal.

In a properly performed tongue piercing, blood loss should be very slight. However, the underneath of the tongue is very busy with veins and arteries and should be thoroughly checked for a vein running up the centre of the tongue. Most people have the veins and arteries running up the sides of the tongue, but some have them up the middle and are quite pronounced. <u>Do Not Attempt To Pierce</u> tongues that present this way, as it can cause severe bleeding. I like to use surgical plastic (PTFE) in mouth piercings.

After the piercing, always advice the client to come back after 2 weeks for a smaller

159

Body Piercing For Students

barbell (downsizing) otherwise there is a chance they may bite on the barbell and chip their teeth.

TONGUE JEWELLERY SELECTION

Curved or Straight barbell 14 gauge

Length 18- 22 mm

Downsize after 3-4 weeks to usually 16 mm straight barbell

TRAY SET UP TONGUE

1. Mouthwash in cup (diluted with water)You need two off.

2. Two cups for spitting into

3. Jewellery

4. Clamps/Forceps

5. Hemostats

6. Scissors

7. Cotton pads 2 small 2 large

8. Gauze

9. Ice Pack

10. Paper towel

11. Dental Chain

12. Camera.

13. Calipers {disposable.}

PROCEDURE FOR TONGUE

After setting up your trolley be sure it is by your side.

I. Check clients tongue for veins/arteries. If vein is present in middle of tongue, do not go ahead with piercing.

2. Make sure their tongue is long enough — get them to stick it out. If too short (cannot get tongue past bottom lip) do not pierce.

3. Check thickness of tongue with venire callipers. Most tongues are 9-11 mm thick

Body Piercing For Students

4. Check position of frenuluin. This should never be pierced.

5. Get them to rinse mouth thoroughly with Mouth wash prior to piercing.

6. Place paper towel on like a bib with dental chain.

7. Mark tongue (with a disposable non toxic pen). The piercing is usually performed approx. 8-15 mm from the tip. Get client to place tongue back in mouth and ask them to open up and you will see where it will sit in position Do not mark too far back on the tongue.

7a. Now apply 2-3 squirts of xylocaine to tongue area and wait 1 minute for it to activate. *However, I strongly recommend you do not do this. The tongue becomes numb and they could easily bit it off. This section is an international standard that I am trying to have abolished. If you do xylocaine the tongue they must stay in the salon until the xylocaine wears off.*

Body Piercing For Students

8. Ask them to stick their tongue out as far as possible and clamp the tongue
Remember tongues are slippery and move a lot so keep a firm grip on the clamps.

9. Sometimes the client can assist the piercing by using their index fingers to pull back on both sides of their lips so they are out of the way of the needle (if they have big lips).

10. Make the piercing from the top of the tongue and make sure the IV cannula is thoroughly sticking out of the base of the tongue.

11. Cut cannula. Place another set of forceps alongside the cannula and remove forceps.

12. Insert Jewellery from bottom to top and secure bead on top. Make sure gloves are dry and screw bead on tightly. It is advisable to hold the jewellery with Hemostats.

13. Check piercing for bleeding and position. Ask that they gently open their

mouth so you can have a look. They may not be able to lift their tongue up or out.

14. Offer a cup for spitting.

15. Give them the diluted mouth wash to gargle.

16. Give them the spit cup and a piece of paper towel

Note: ALWAYS have your client lie down after the piercing and keep an eye on them. I take their pulse before and after the piercing and make a note on their client sheet.

DOWNSIZING: Don't rush. Is the first thing you need to tell the client. Ensure that tongue swelling has completely subsided. If satisfied, remove initial barbell and insert new one from underneath tongue and screw bead on top. Check it is not too tight, leaving at least 1 mm on either side. Get client to rinse with Listerine afterwards.

The tongue is shaped like a triangle wide at the base and tapering almost to a point at its tip. It is attached at its base to the lower jaw and to the mandible. At its sides the root is joined to the walls of the pharynx, the cavity that forms the back of the mouth. The middle part of the tongue has a curved upper surface, while its lower surface is connected to the floor of the mouth by a thin strip of tissue, the FRENULUM.

The muscle fibres in the Tongue run up and down and side to side. The tongues actions are given a huge versatility by the contractions from a variety of muscles that are situated in the neck and side of the jaws. The styloglossus muscle in the neck brings the tongue up and back and the hyoglossus brings it back down.

Body Piercing For Students

NOSTRIL JEWELLERY

Jewellery Type ….Nostril Screws, CBR's 810 mm, Nose Studs" L" shaped do not use nose studs that have more than one bend in them. They hurt going in and are prone to moving when the client breathes heavy. Avoid Nose Studs with jewels for the initial piercing and nose studs that have an S bend in them.

NOSTRIL TRAY SET

Clean the tray and cover with two layers of paper towel, place on tray:

1. IV Cannula Needle 16 to 18 gauge to match Jewellery size

2. Gloves that fit tight

3. Container with Betadine

4. Place the jewellery in container

Body Piercing For Students

5. Needle receiving tube or cork however if you're using an IV cannula needle you will not need a receiving tube.

6. Small Forceps

7. Scissors

8. Cotton bud

9. Marker Pen

10. Alcohol swab

11. 4 cotton wool swabs

12. Paper Towel

13. Dental chain to hold paper towel around clients neck

14. Head band to place around clients hair

15. A few tissues.

16. Ice on Gauze.

17. Camera

Clients Position

Body Piercing For Students

Client is sitting up on the bed. NOT A CHAIR. Be sure client can be put into the prone position quickly if they faint or bleed heavily.

PROCEDURE NOSTRIL

You wash hands and put on gloves.

1. Clean The Nose. Be sure they give their nose a good blow into a tissue one nostril at a time. Use Betadine on cotton pad to clean the nose.

2. Mark the position

3. Have the client check and affirm they are happy with the position otherwise clean the nose again and remark a position pleasing to them. Then check that is a good position for the piercing.

4. Take a photo.

5. Position the forceps and pinch the site.

6. Angle the needle at ninety degrees and pierce into a receiving tube. Very quickly pull the needle out leaving the cannula in the nose.

7. Cut the top of the cannula.

8. Remove the forceps. Use two fingers to pinch each side of the cannula.

9. Remove the forceps.

10. Place jewellery into the tube of the cannula. As you push jewellery through, pull cannula out of the nose from the inside of the nose.

11. Care for Client.

12. Have them place their hands behind their head.

13. Apply gentle pressure with a cotton swab and ice..

14. Clean the site with saline.

15. That their pulse and be sure they are in a safe state of mind before they leave. If their pulse is normal clean

the piercing have them relax. Give them an ice block.

16. Extended care. Set a date for them to return for their check up

17. Go through their aftercare with them.

~~~~ *** ~~~~

NAVEL TRAY SETUP

Special Considerations

The client should ideally have a well shaped/ fonned upper piece of tissue hanging down in a crescent formation. In a classic 'vertical' navel piercing, the jewellery hangs straight down from the upper fold. The success rate is highest on clients with deep navels which has a pronounced fold. This does not mean that shallow navels are not able to be pierced. It simply means that extra care must be taken to ensure the piercing heals well and stays in place. If the client has a large or deep navel a 12 mm curved jewellery should be used.

NAVEL JEWELLERY SELECTION

Curved barbell

Gauge 14

Length 10-12 mm

TRAY SETUP NAVEL

1. Cotton buds

2. Betadine in a kidney bowl

3. Needle 14g LV cannula

4. Jewellery 14g 10 mm long Banana Navel Bar for large bodies use 12 mm Jewellery

5. Forceps

6. Hemostats

7. Scissors

8. Rubber band

9. Marking pen

10. Non adhesive pad. (square bandage)

Body Piercing For Students

11. Gauze

12. Masking tape

13. Ice Pack

14. Camera

PROCEDURE NAVEL

1. Swab area with Proviodine Iodine. Or Betadine.

2. Have client stand.

3. Mark entrance and exit points. Normally 8 mm or 10 mm on a larger person. Always mark 2 mm shy of the Jewellery size to allow for swelling.

4. Once the client has approved the site position take a photo and have then sign the from.

5. Place rubber band on forceps to obtain tighter tension. (optional)

6. Place forceps on navel and pierce from top to bottom.

7. Cut cannula off at the base.

8. Pinch site each side of forceps.

9. Remove forceps.

10. Thread Jewellery through the cannula while holding the pinch. Be sure you have a tight pinch on the site as you remove the cannula.

11. If using a barbell, thread Jewellery through from the bottom, holding flesh firmly with Gauze so as not to lose the piercing, remove catheter and screw ball on top of barbell.

12. Ask client to place their hands above their head and take their pulse.

13. Place an ice pack over the piecing and apply pressure.

14. Once bleeding has ceased, cover the area with a non adhesive pad. This prevents blood staining the client's clothes, as it can leak over the next 10 minutes due to movement. Advise the client it can be removed in 1 hour

and to simply wash with warm water to remove any dried blood.

15. Tell client to cover with a waterproof bandage when they go swimming and not to dry it with a towel.

16. They must wear loose fitting clothes during the healing period.

17. Set up a date for their check-up within the next three days.

18. Take a photo.

~~~**~~~

Note. All photos must be added to the clients forms and filed under the clients name .

NEEDLE GAUGE

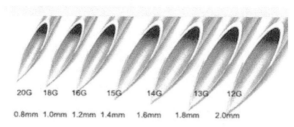

When using a cannula needle the gauge is of the cannula and the actual needle will be one size smaller.

Guage ▾	Gauge ▾	Diameter ▾
Uk-Europe	USA	MM
1.0mm	18ga	6mm
1.2mm	16ga	8mm
2.00mm	14ga	10mm
2.4mm	10ga	11mm
3.2mm	8ga	12mm

BALL GAUGE CONVERSION

Millimetres	Inches
3	1/8
4	5/32
5	3/16
6	1/4
8	5/16
10	3/8

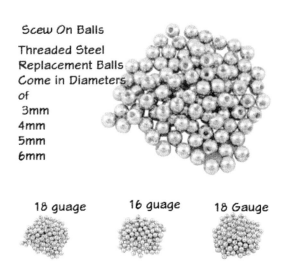

Scew On Balls

Threaded Steel
Replacement Balls
Come in Diameters
of
 3mm
4mm
5mm
6mm

18 guage   16 guage   18 Gauge

Body Piercing For Students

HEALING TIMES

Ear Lobe Between 4-8 weeks

Ear Rim Between 2-4 months

Eye Brow Between 2-4 months

Tongue Between 2-3 months

Labret Between 2-4 months

Nipple Between 2-6 months

Lips Between 2-4 months

Nostril Between 2-4 months

Navel Between 3-12 months

Body Piercing For Students

Healing Time Chart

Earlobe:	4-8 Weeks
· Septum:	4-8 Weeks
· Female Nipple:	2-6 Months
· Frenum:	2-3 Months
· Apadravya:	4-10 Months
· Clitoral Hood:	2-3 Months
· Christina:	2-3 Months
· Monroe:	2-3 Months
· Ear Cartilage:	2-12 Months
· Eyebrow:	2-3 Months
· Navel:	4-12 Months
· Scrotum:	2-3 Months
· Dydoe:	2-6 Months
· Inner Labia:	4-8 Weeks
· Tongue:	3-4 Weeks
· Nostril:	2-6 Months
· Male Nipple:	2-3 Months
· Prince Albert:	4-6 Weeks
· Ampallang:	6-10 Months
· Guiche:	2-3 Months
· Outer Labia:	3-6 Months
· Lip:	6-12 Weeks
· Labret:	6-12 Weeks
· Handweb: ...	8-12 Weeks

PMMA
POLYMETHYLMETHACRYLATE:

This Polymer, better known as acrylic is increasingly used, in medical situations, and its suitability for body jewellery is widely acknowledged. Anecdotal and empirical evidence indicates that the human body tolerates acrylics exceptionally well.

PMMA was one of the first plastics to be developed in the second and third decades of the twentieth century. It was successfully employed as a substitute for glass in windscreens for motor vehicles and aeroplanes. PMMA became subsequently the material of choice for contact lenses, cosmetic surgery and spinal fixation devices. Considered biologically inert, PMMA is better known under its various brand names. Lucite, Plexiglass, Perspex.

No Wildcat Fluoro reactive pieces will strip away from threaded metal posts like many products of similar lines. PMMA pieces are threaded in the PMMA itself providing a more solid product.

Body Piercing For Students

UNDERSTANDING SUPPLIERS CODES

These days most suppliers have a photo next to or under the code. In the next photo I have put a red square or circle around the

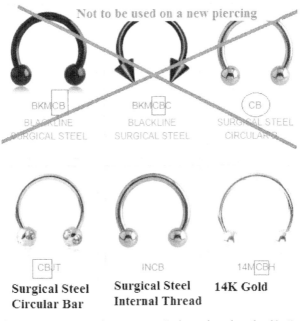

letters CB . These are "circular barbells".

Body Piercing For Students

In the next photo the red circle is around "BC" these are called "Ball Closure Ring " or some suppliers call them "Captive Beads" because they capture the two ends of the bar to close and become a closed circle.

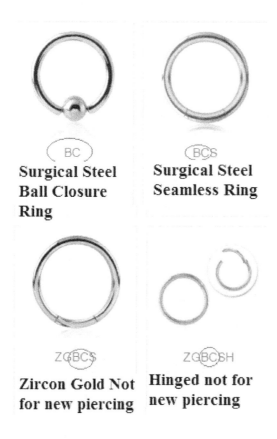

BC

Surgical Steel Ball Closure Ring

BCS

Surgical Steel Seamless Ring

ZGBCS

Zircon Gold Not for new piercing

ZGBCSH

Hinged not for new piercing

Body Piercing For Students

However, as you can see in the next photo Sleepers are also listed on the Ball Capture pages even though they do not have a ball.

When you first start in the industry the suppliers terminology can be confusing.

I have listed a suppliers catalogue page for you to have a look at.

https://www.piercingsupplies.com.au

Contact them and ask for a catalogue to be sent to you. However some suppliers will not do this for students you actually need to be a salon owner. You can order jewellery from many other retailers and there is loads of jewellery on EBay.

Warning. You need to order jewellery that has a code 316L after the statement "Surgical Steel" 346L certified.

This should be enough information for you to now start researching what the different types of jewellery are called.

During your Body Piercing course you will be required to place a jewellery order or at least set up an order sheet. You can request order sheets from most suppliers. They are usually more than happy to send you an order form. Once you have that you can ask the appropriate questions about their codes. As you read through this book things you need to know about jewellery will become clearer.

PTFE:

PTFE: Another of my favourite piercing material and should be favoured by Piercers because of the fast healing times and by piercing fans who experience reaction to certain metals or alloys.
Polytetrafluoroethylene is an astonishing implantable thermoplastic polymer which has amazing inertness and excellent biocompatibility characteristics. Due to the tendency of PTFE molecules to repel other molecules, the material exhibits phenomenal "non stick" properties. The coefficient of friction of PTFE is less than that of ice. It is unaffected by most chemical environments and it is very

difficult for any material to bond to it. PTFE is often used by Surgeons for small volume implants in facial reconstruction, middle ear surgery and large diameter blood vessel replacements. A new surgical dimension has been a liquidized version of PTFE being used as a blood substitute, due to its super light weight.

 PTFE body Jewellery is being strongly favoured by Piercers because of dramatically fast healing times and by piercing fans that experience reaction to certain metals or alloys. PTFE is also flexible. Charge extra for PTFE. Advertise your piercings at $79 with the option of PTFE for $15 more. There are many reasons why Jewellers have a high mark up on jewellery. That will be explained on your practical day. Rule of thumb is Cost plus tax plus delivery times 6.

Lets say the jewellery costs you $5. Delivery on 100 items was $30. That is only $5.30 but you also have to consider:-

♣ The time it took to order

Body Piercing For Students

- The tax

- Insurance for theft and other forms of insurance

- Do you need to place it in a showcase? If yes that showcase is using space and space costs money. It may need lights in the showcase and you need staff to sell the item.

That is why you need to multiply the cost by six.

If it costs $5.30 and .53 cents tax

$5.83 x 6 = $34.98

Thirty five dollars fifty ($35.50) is what you need to sell it for to cover your costs and to be able to order more stock. If you have light fingered staff or stock sometimes just disappears you should be charging about $39 for that piece of jewellery if you want to stay in business and be able to pay all your running costs.

JEWELLERY SAFETY METALS - BODY PIERCING.

Not all Jewellery is suitable for a fresh piercing. Remember the dangerous components for us humans are alloys such as nickel, lead, mercury, aluminium, copper, brass etc. Asian Silver has Nickel added as it's a hardener metal yet it cannot be used as a body piercing metal in body piercing jewellery as it contaminates the skin and causes the piercing hole to go black in colour.

The problems with these alloys are that our body (mainly our liver) does not have the ability to flush them out of our systems, so they accumulate and start causing long term, mild to serious, health breakdowns. Fatigue, skin eruptions, lack lustre hair and general loss of humour, bad temper and mood swings can be experienced. "Feeling liverish" is the general expression you've probably heard. With surgical stainless steel (316 L grade is important) the alloys being leeched out the quality from Asia is usually 316 grade it's the" L" for leeched that makes the difference. Asia doesn't leech their metals.

Do not put the following metals into your new piercing until it is well healed:

STERLING SILVER, UV, ACRYLIC, GOLD PLATED, 9 CT GOLD OR FEATURE BARS WITH SILVER OR ACRYLIC, PICTURES (SMILEY FACES ETC)

By law, all Jewellery must be sterilized before being placed into a fresh piercing. Clients should always ask their piercer if the Jewellery has been sterilized.

Remember always to check the quality of safety and wearability e.g. Bright and shiny, no machine marks or scratches, no sharp edges, sufficient thread in Barbells (at least four turns and a tight close down to lock ball on).

Body Piercing For Students

JEWELLERY TYPES

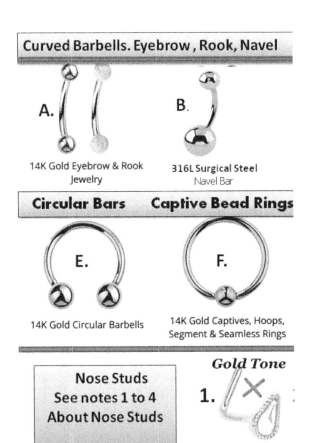

Curved Barbells. Eyebrow, Rook, Navel

A.

B.

14K Gold Eyebrow & Rook
Jewelry

316L Surgical Steel
Navel Bar

Circular Bars **Captive Bead Rings**

E.

F.

14K Gold Circular Barbells

14K Gold Captives, Hoops,
Segment & Seamless Rings

Nose Studs
See notes 1 to 4
About Nose Studs

Gold Tone

1.

Body Piercing For Students

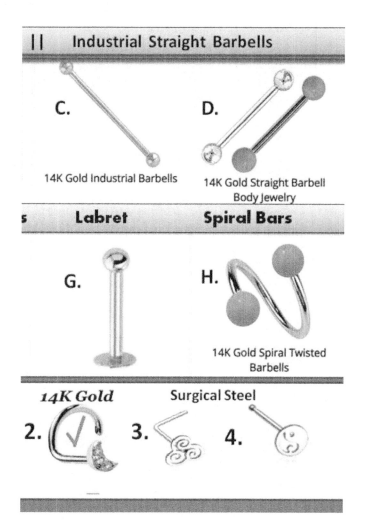

II **Industrial Straight Barbells**

C.

14K Gold Industrial Barbells

D.

14K Gold Straight Barbell
Body Jewelry

s **Labret**   **Spiral Bars**

G.

H.

14K Gold Spiral Twisted
Barbells

14K Gold   Surgical Steel

2.   **3.**   **4.**

Body Piercing For Students

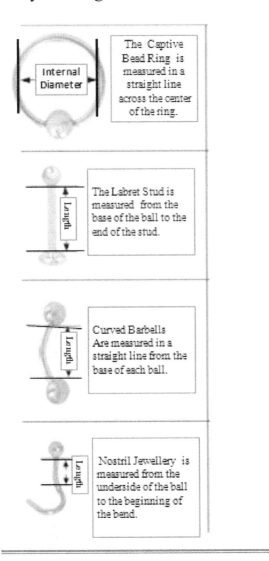

The Captive Bead Ring is measured in a straight line across the center of the ring.

The Labret Stud is measured from the base of the ball to the end of the stud.

Curved Barbells Are measured in a straight line from the base of each ball.

Nostril Jewellery is measured from the underside of the ball to the beginning of the bend.

Body Piercing For Students

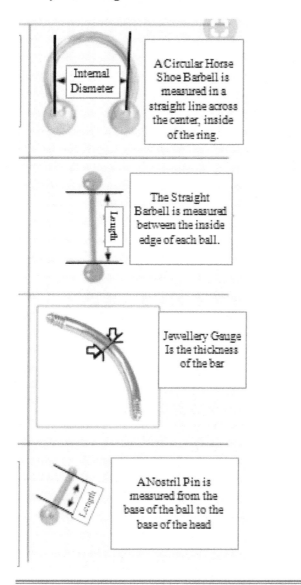

A Circular Horse Shoe Barbell is measured in a straight line across the center, inside of the ring.

The Straight Barbell is measured between the inside edge of each ball.

Jewellery Gauge Is the thickness of the bar

A Nostril Pin is measured from the base of the ball to the base of the head

January Garnet — February Amethyst — March Aquamarine — April Diamond

May Emerald — June Pearl — July Ruby — August Peridot

September Sapphire — October Tourmaline — November Topaz — December Turquoise

NOTE ON NOSE STUDES

See above jewellery photo

1. Never use gold tone jewellery in a new piercing. The shape in the photo above is excellent for a new piercing.

2 14 and 18k solid gold is excellent for a new piercing but the shape is hard to push in.

Body Piercing For Students

3. & 4. Surgical steel is perfect for new piercings. Both the shape of 3 and 4 are easy to place in a new nostril piercing.

The safest nose stud for a new piercing is bio-plast

Nose Studs
Bio-plast

SALINE SOLUTION RECIPE

For home use, to be applied as an alternative healing solution for Body Piercings.

Mix quarter a teaspoon of Deep Sea salt (not Iodised Salt) into one litre of **BOILED** water. Store in a clean, lidded container (that has been washed out with boiling water)

Remember less salt is best, more salt irritates the piercing. Store in a airtight clean jar and keep in a cupboard.

Renew solution every three days. Apply twice daily after washing hands or showering. Rotate the ring or move the Jewellery up and down as you apply the saline solution. **Do Not** move the Jewellery at any other time as it will prolong the healing process.

Dry the area well after cleaning with a fresh piece of cotton wool _Not Your Towel_

Body Piercing For Students

Use Saline Solution only in this specific formula. If the solution is too strong it may dry and burn the wound.

Do not use Saline as supplied for Contact Lenses as it contains other chemicals which may hinder good healing.

Consult your Body Piercer or Doctor if you have any concerns about healing. Vitamins C or Zinc Tablets will also aid healing. We recommend Aromatherapy healers to be sprayed or dabbed onto the pierced area.

Warning: never ever use ointment, balms or salve on your piercing as it is an open wound and the ointment will go into your blood stream and settle in your liver. It stays there causing problems later on in your life.

Body Piercing For Students

A painless piercing means a quick healing.

1. While the client is filling in their form set up your tray.

2. Wash your hands with an antibacterial soap.

1. Put on tight fitting gloves.

2. Lay three pieces of white paper towel onto the piercing tray. Set the tray up and cover with white paper towel.

3. Place the needle the jewellery and other items as per the set ups instructions for each type of piercing.

4. Take the ball off the jewellery or open the captive bead.

5. Place the jewellery into a cup with Betadine or Alcohol. Both are great antiseptics but must be wiped off before inserting the jewellery, as they

are not designed for internal use. You are going to be piercing a hole in your clients flesh.

6. Change to a clean pair of surgical gloves before attending to the clients piercing.

7. Wipe/clean the piercing position on the client with an alcohol swab then apply Betadine.

8. Measure the area with your callipers. Put a dot where the needle will go in and where it will come out. If the jewellery is 10 mm long or 10 mm in diameter then you measure 8 mm between dots. This will allow for swelling. We are talking about millimetres. **They are tiny distances yet one millimetre out can cause many problems.**

9. Put the piercing tray on a trolley close to where you are going to stand. You do not want to reach for the ball and find the tray is not close enough.

Body Piercing For Students

10.Be sure you have taken the needle out of the sealed wrap and moved the cannula to be sure it does not stick. You should show the needle to the client first so they are sure you are using a sterilized needle. Sometimes the cannula has a burr in it. You need to check the cannula to be sure it is smooth. If it has a burr it will not go through the skin. I have seen a cannula pleat like a tiny fan on the insertion point of a piercing just because the student went like a bat out of hell and did not check the cannula for burrs.

11.For a mouth piercing Tongue/Beauty spot/labret give them a diluted mouthwash and have them spit into a plastic cup wipe their mouth with paper towel. Put the paper towel in the spit cup and put into the bin.

12.Place the forceps on one dot that can be viewed clearly in the middle of the forceps use your fingers to pinch the skin and line up the other dot with the other side of the forceps.

13. Keep the forceps firmly pinched together or put a rubber band on the forceps to help with the firmness of the pinch.

14. If using professional forceps be sure not to lock the locking clip this will cause phenomenal pain.

15. Push the needle through very quickly and remove the needle leaving the cannula (plastic tube) in.

16. While the forceps are still on you firmly pinch the skin close to the forceps before removing the forceps.

17. Use your fingers to pinch the piercing very close to where the needle entered the skin. Pinch as close to the cannula as possible.

18. Keep that pinch tight and remove the forceps.

19. Cut the cannula a little shorter but not too short. Do not slacked your pinch as the skin cells will move and cause great pain. One end of the cannula is smaller than the other. If this is the end the jewellery is to go in that is the end you must cut.

20. Keep that pinch tight while removing the forceps. If you forget to remove the forceps now the ball may not fit through the loop of the forceps and you will have to take the jewellery out of the piercing and re-pierce.

21. Keep that pinch tight and push the jewellery through the center tunnel of the cannula.

22. Do not move your fingers that are pinching the skin. Now put some other fingers on the jewellery to prevent it from moving. If it is a mouth piercing use cotton gauze to keep the jewellery in place while you put the ball on the jewellery.

23. Screw the ball into place or put the captive bead in place. Keep that jewellery and the skin well pinched and put the ball on the jewellery. You should have such a tight pinch on the skin and jewellery that the jewellery does not move. If the jewellery moves while putting on the ball the pain will be excruciating /agonizing.

Furthermore the skin cells will not form a clean cylinder shape around the jewellery and may cause a Keloid to form within the next few months. There is no known cure for a Keloid.

The skin cells that you cannot see are all in shock and trying to rush to the wound to close the hole. They are very busy so you are trying to create a trick so Mother Nature does not want to beat you to the hole. Even a slight movement at this time will cause great pain. All the cells have divided into lots of smaller cells. A less painful piercing means you have done a good job and the healing time will be shorter.

24. Ask the client to put their hands above their head.

25. Hold cotton wool dipped in saline on the piercing and apply pressure for one minute.

26. Add the cold gauze to give some relief.

27. After a few minutes put their hands down and take their pulse. Be sure they are not feeling anxious before they leave the salon..

28. You can now have a chat but never ever chat during the piercing and never ever allow another person in your piercing room.

29. Give them a drink while still sitting on the bed. If they have had a mouth piercing Tongue/Labret/Beauty spot give them some ice or an iceblock.

30.Make an appointment for them to return in 3 to 4 days time. Then make an appointment for the week after so you can clean the piercing professionally and check up on their aftercare routine and their healing process.

31.Be sure to give them a small bag of deep sea salt and an aftercare sheet or an Aromatherapy aftercare solution.

Note: For a mouth piercing they will need to rinse their mouth out with diluted mouth wash as soon as the jewellery has gone in then you would apply pressure with a saline soaked single use cloth. Then apply the Ice pack or give them an ice block.

Body Piercing For Students

YOUR DO'S AND DON'TS OUTLINED

Cleanliness Is Next to Godliness

1. Always clean your bed, trolley, benches and sink with disinfectant. Including, the frame and legs of the bed.

2. Never ever put a cloth, towel or cover on your bed.

3. Do not have curtains in the room

4. Do not have air conditioner going during the piercing. Use a fan if the weather is hot and uncomfortable so germs do not enter the air conditioner.

5. Have everything in a cupboard and never have the cupboard open while you are doing a piercing. Everything in the cupboard should be in air tight containers or plastic zip bags.

6. If you have things such as cotton pads and other items on a bench be sure they are in tightly sealed jars.

7. Wipe the jars and bench over after a piercing. Use disinfectant and paper towels.

8. Be sure your paper towel is in a sealed container too.

9. Be sure you wear a disposable plastic gown, cap, boots and mask as well as your gloves.

10. Spray the room with disinfectant after the piercing and keep the door shut.

11. Use a pedal bin.

12. Use taps that you flick on with your elbow.

13. Wash hands before and after the piercing.

14. Place all throw away items in the bin. Open the bin with your foot on the pedal.

15. Do not wear socks or stockings. If you do; cover with disposable plastic boots. I always wear the plastic boots once I enter the dedicated piercing room. I remove them before I remove my gloves and before I leave the room.

16. Place your tools in a container that has a lid and a disinfectant solution.

17. Put your needle in the sharps container. When the container is almost full, put some plaster in the sharps container and some water shake and allow to set hard. Give sharps container to your local doctor. Some towns had a free drop off depo and some towns have a pickup service. Do not put the container in your rubbish bin.

18. Scrub your tools with disinfectant and washing soap or green soap and a toothbrush that you throw away after each use. Rinse under running water

in a dedicated scrubs sink. Dry with
white paper towel.

19. Place each tool in an open position
and place in an autoclave bag. If you
do not have an autoclave take the
tools in the bags to your Doctor,
Dentist or the local hospital. They
will charge around $5 to autoclave
for you.

20. There is a tag on the autoclave bag
that needs to be placed inside the
bag. The tag will change colour when
the tools have completed the
sterilization in the autoclave.

21. Be sure to have them sign your
book.

22. Measles, mumps, chickenpox, the
flue and other diseases can also, be
spread around your salon. The client
may not know they have it at the time
of a piercing and they may have
been in contact with a carrier of a
disease.

23. Your piercing room should be, treated as a surgeon would treat his/her operating theatre.

24. Always be cautious and be exceptionally clean.

25. Never ever use slang. In your 'Code Of Conduct' it tells you to never ever use slang, nor say yep, yer, nup.

26. Always dress in all black or all white outfits.

27. Where a plastic gown over your clothes during the piercing and remove before leaving the piercing room.

28. Where nurses shoes or leather shoes, not cloth shoes.

29. Put plastic covers over your shoes and remove before leaving the piercing room.

30. Put your protective clothing in the pedal bin when you have completed the piercing. But, not before the room

has been completely cleaned and sprayed with antiseptic.

31. Refer to the person as a client not a customer. Retail outlets have customers professional with a diploma or above have clients.

STERILIZATION

Sterilization must be recorded in a book and kept in the piercing room.

When the tools go into the autoclave bag so must the tag on the bag.

The autoclave bag must be dated and the name of the item written on the bag.

In the sterilization book:-

Date Item Scrubbed by

Autoclaved by Date& Sign

The date they were scrubbed

The name of the item e.g. forceps or Hemostats, scissors, and so on.

Body Piercing For Students

Who scrubbed them on that date?

Where were they autoclaved and by whom.

Signed and dated by the Autoclave person
when you pick them up or take them out of
your autoclave.

Peel Off Tag

FINAL TEST

1. What are the seven secret to becoming a Professional Body Piercer.

2. What will make you a better Body Piercer than the rest of the piercers in your area? Give no more than one page of information here?

3. Should it be Ok if you use slang sometimes?

4. Will you get most of your supplies from two main suppliers?

5. Name all the piercing above waist? Hint there are at least 13 piercing on the ear.

6. If you are trained in Body Piercing under the Beauty Therapy Australian Standards and add one more Beauty Code to your skills your insurance for your entire business will be $400 $900 per year. What will be your insurance cost if you are not trained this way and want to add tongue and dermal piercings to your insurance? Give quotes from three insurance companies.

Body Piercing For Students

7. What are diseases that can stay in your piercing room if you do not clean and spray the room correctly? Name six.

8. Now add two Anatomy photos of each above waist piercing.

ANATOMY AND CONTRA-INDICATIONS

This book is not about learning all there is to know about skin biology, anatomy nor all the contraindications. This is a basic introduction into body piercing. Further studies may be required by some students.

NERVES OF THE FACE

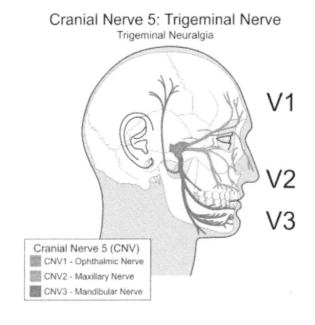

Cranial Nerve 5: Trigeminal Nerve
Trigeminal Neuralgia

V1

V2

V3

Cranial Nerve 5 (CNV)
CNV1 - Ophthalmic Nerve
CNV2 - Maxillary Nerve
CNV3 - Mandibular Nerve

Body Piercing For Students

Have a look on the internet for a clearer picture of the Nerves of the face and have it enlarged. Then laminate it and put on the wall in your piercing room. It is important to know where the nerves around the eyebrow are and to avoid piercing through a ophthalmic nerve. Slowly pinch along the intended site and gain clients reaction before marking the placement.

INVERTED NIPPLE

Anatomy of the Female Breast

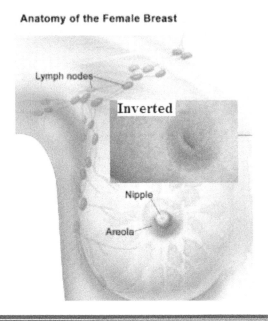

Body Piercing For Students

You need to use ice and a friction massage method to get the inverted nipple to stand proud before a nipple piercing.

Best Jewellery for body piercing is considered to be Surgical Steele 316L.

You need to be sure that is what you are purchasing .Surgical Steel and steel look the same. Some clients will have an allergic reaction to Surgical Steele. Titanium is less reactive , yet more expensive. Titanium however is often coated with an anodized paint that melts into the blood stream.

Black Steele should never, be used in a new piercing and you need to be careful when purchasing black Steele that it is what it is and not coloured metal. That is why I purchase my coloured Jewellery such as black Steele from AAB Fashions because what they say the material is that is what it is. Other suppliers may be as honest but these are the ones that I trust. However, always check as suppliers do change ownership and rules go flying out the window.

Body Piercing For Students

At this point I recommend you buy my Body Piercing Bible it has photos of things that go wrong in the piercing room and how to fix those things.

You are far safer to do new piercings in PTFE as that is the plastic that Doctors use.

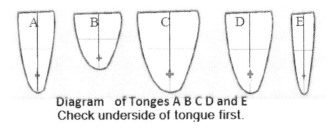

Diagram of Tonges A B C D and E
Check underside of tongue first.

WHERE TO PIERCE THE TONGUE

Tongue shapes red + indicates where to do the piercing.

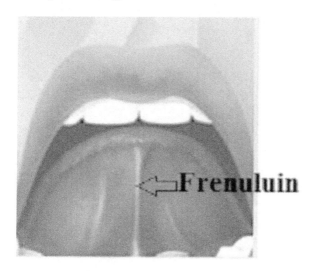

This person cannot have a tongue piercing. Her frenuluin is too thick and runs the full length of the tongue. He/ She would become speech impaired.

Mouth Anatomy

Search for more diagrams on the anatomy of the tongue. It is very important with piercings to know what is beneath the skin.

~~~ * ~~~

CONTRA-INDICATION

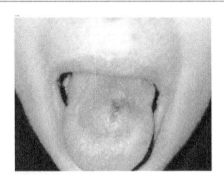

TONGUE

This persons jewellery was probably too short and did not allow for swelling. It was pierced too far back on the tongue.

The piercer probably was not trained in Anatomy. The piercer did not I assume have the client return for a check up 3-5 days after they did this piercing.

The client used a mouthwash that had not been diluted and probably is a smoker. If they cannot give up smoking for a week then they should not have a tongue nor a labret piercing.

NAVEL INFECTION.

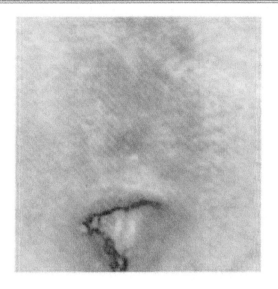

This client was pierced with the wrong size jewellery and the in and out positions where too far apart. This person had a lovely navel and now has to have plastic surgery to fix the perturbing navel. Some of the scars will heal with Aromatherapy but the protrusion needs surgery.

EAR PIERCING WITH A GUN

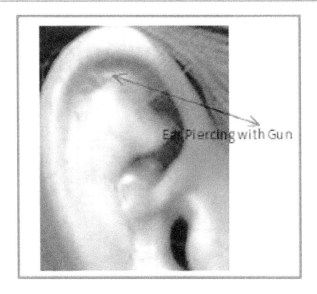

This person was pierced with a gun in a hairdressing salon. Cart ledges of the ear cannot be pierced with a gun. She will have that scar forever.

WRONG JEWELLERY

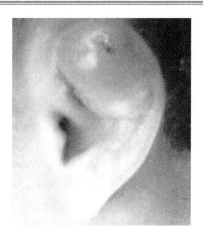

This person was allergic to the surgical steel. It was a double piercing to house a ring and the jewellery was too small in diameter. Do not try to remove this send a person like this to the doctors. Give them some ice in a plastic bag wrapped in paper towel. Tell them to hold it on the piercing and go straight to the doctors.

How do I know the jewellery was the wrong type she said her ear was burning within an hour? She rang her body piercer and was told that is natural. Her ear went like this within 4 days. Now do you see

221

why it is very important that they return to you within a few days for a check up?

If they travel for over an hour to get to work they may not be able to see you until their next day off. Tell them you are happy for a web-conference if they have any concerns. Call them three days after the piercing and ask a few questions.

Now research body piercing contraindications on Google.

Body piercing is moderately, contraindicated in individuals with the following conditions or circumstances: A family or personal history of keloid scarring, especially if over 11 years of age. Valvular heart disease — for oral piercings. Uncontrolled, bleeding disorder.

There are a huge number of contraindications, caused by the clients aftercare, allergic reactions' to alcohol wipes, metals and other items used in the piercing room. Allergic reactions can be either mild and fixable or fatale and for this reason you need to know them. Study never

ever ends. Not even after you have your certificate.

CHECK ON YOUR CLIENT

The day after the client has had a piercing call and check on them. Ask the client how they feel and check how the piercing feels.

Does the piercing site feel cool or very warm?

Is there any sensation such as burning stinging or pain?

If "no" to all these questions check what they are doing to keep the swelling down and check how they are cleaning it.

If everything sounds fine, good, wait until they have a day off. But, if they say they have any of the warning signals then stay back and wait for them to come home from work to assist them. You do not want your salons name on the world wide web, name and shame list. The more particular you are the better. People will spread the word that you are caring and particular.

Body Piercing For Students

Client follow ups and client after service care is what builds a business and good reputations.

When the client returns to a check-up if the piercing is stinging or very hot:

Apply ice for twenty minutes or ask them to apply the ice straight away and come to the salon as quickly as they can.

Apply ELMA cream around the piercing not on it. Wait for the ELMA cream to work this takes about forty to sixty minutes.

As you remove the jewellery, push the jewellery out with a PTFE pierce of jewellery. Do not remove it and then try to push the new jewellery through. Do not remove jewellery if they have pus. However replace the jewellery with a larger size if they are swollen but only after a 20 minute ice pack has been applied. When the swelling has subsides apply the ELMA cream and wait for it to work.

ELMA CREAM FINDINGS

Read this info on ELMA cream

http://xpil.medicines.org.uk/ViewPil.aspx?
DocID=3478

PIERCINGS POSITIONS

Under the Beauty Standard of Australia there are 13 ear positions, plus 3 nose positions - nostril, septum, nose bridge, 1 position for eyebrow, beauty spot, labret, tongue, nipple and navel. There are twenty two above waist piercings outlined in the Australian and International Standards. All other piercings are not covered in the Standards. Therefore, the insurance for Dermal and Genital piercings may not be covered by your insurance. It is important to note that although Tongue piercings, maybe covered in your training it is often not covered by insurance companies.

Be sure you have set up a "Tray Setup:" protocol page for each piercing. Then you must check your setup protocol before you begin a piercing.

Be sure you have a "Procedure" protocol page for each piercing written out for all these piercings. They need to be in your "Piercings Protocols Book".

Then have an abbreviated version for each piercing on an A4 size sheet of paper. On one side is the tray set-up check list. On the other side you have the Procedures.

You then laminate the page for each piercing.

When you set up the room for a client look at the laminated page for the piercing, you are going to do on that client. Place a tick with a sharpie pen next to each item as you place it on the set-up tray. When the tray is ready cover it with paper towel and clean the laminated sheet. Flip the sheet over and read your procedure.

You are making a hole in the body and you need to act like a surgeon. In a piercing room, you do not usually have a nurse to hand you things. Therefore, you need to be very well organized.

The tray needs to be placed on a mobile trolley next to your dominant hand.

The tongue piercings is not usually covered by your insurance so be sure when purchasing insurance that it is covered by the insurance supplier. If they do not cover you then you will need to explain to your client that tongue piercings are not covered and the client needs to sign a disclaimer releasing you from responsibility should something go wrong.

The International Standards was written for above waist piercings only. Dermal piercings and other body modifications have no standards. Therefore, they cannot be part of body piercing insurance. For this reason, you need to have clients sign a disclaimer.

TRAINING CENTRE'S

Beauty School Books and That's Great Distance Learning It is an International Academe that teaches you via web-conference. No matter what country you live in this course can be done via web-Conference.

http://www.beautyschoolbooks.com.au

You need:-

    A. Computer

    B. Web camera on a long cord.

    C. Internet connection

    D. Skype downloaded

    E. Piercings tool

    F. Pork skin

A camera, on a long cord. They will not and cannot accept a camera that is attached to your computer. It must be one on a long cord attached to your computer via a USB cable called a webcam. You need to move the camera into a position so the teacher is able to see your work. However with the advancement of technology you may be able to video chat from your smart phone.

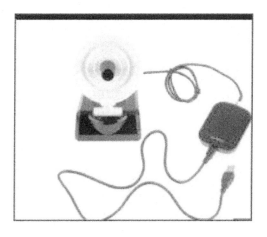

www.beautyschoolbooks.com.au

www.thatsgreat.co

Email beautyschoolbooks@gmail.com

Body Piercing For Students

When looking for a training facility check that they other a full time six week course or longer. They also need to offer you backup and support for at least six months.

SUPPLIERS

Monster Steel

In USA they take about 3 weeks to deliver and delivery is expensive so only use if placing a big order. Also do not order any piercing jewellery unless it is 316L from them. Do not buy their tools for use on clients. But they are cheap for in salon jewellery sales once a piercing has fully healed and they have a large range. www.monstersteel.com

AAB Fashions
www.mojointernational.com

3/27 William St Balclava 3182 Telephone 0395273777

They have tools and jewellery. They answer the telephone every time I ring and they are

Body Piercing For Students

very helpful and they delivery very quickly
99% of the time.

ABK Imports Pty Ltd

 They are reliable and helpful. They have
316L Surgical Steel.
www.abkimports.com.au/

U13/ 18 Strang S, Beaconsfield WA Phone:
1800 633 657

Pierce and Price

www.pierceandprice.com.au....Just
jewellery

Yoop......just jewellery

Bondi Beach Sydney www.yoop.com.au

Livingston Tel: 1300557557 Ask them to
send the Beauty Therapy Brochure.

Needles and medical suppliers. A very large
business hard to communicate with but
when everyone else runs out they have
supplies.

Body Piercing For Students

Well the list of suppliers I have dealt with is endless but these are the ones I know and trust and use all the time.

Associations

Association of Professional Australian Aestheticians

PHONE: 07 5575 9364 | EMAIL: info@apaa.com.au | www.apaa.com.au

P.O Box 96 Robina QLD 4226

I also am a member of APAA. They have been in business now for 52 years so they are doing something right. Their website is loaded with adverts and they are the ones that the Government asked to write the Australian Standards In 1992 and then they commissioned myself and many other therapists to assist with the setting up of the Australian standards. Their joining fee is around $70 and yearly about $255. To become a member means you can use the initials APAA after your name on your business card and place a poster outside your Salon telling people you are a professional ruled by a code of ethics.

Body Piercing For Students

I trust you found this book helpful. Many thanks for your decision to own this manual.

OTHER BOOKS BY ROBYNA SMITH-KEYS

Healing And Training Manuals

Foolproof Aromatherapy

Essential oils can heal, sooth and energise. Learn how to mix. When not to use and all the benefits for hundreds of ailments listed in alphabetical order. User friendly.

The Antique Healer

This is a much large Aromatherapy book with photos and more healings. Also contains wise old women's remedies. To be release 2016

I Was Not Ready To Lose My Mother

My mother had a few weeks to live. Her Cancer was very aggressive.I set her up on a healing program of juices, essential oils and herbs. This was all working until she stopped the program. It also has a lovely story about her life. Married at age 16 until her Passover.

Body Piercing For Students

Note this book is not completed yet but I have taken a small section of this book and uploaded it to Kindle and Smashwords.Called:-

Organic Cancer Cure.

A brief to the point book on how my mother lived a few more years after being told she had a few days to a couple of weeks to live. Not only did she get a few more years but she regained her quality of life.We used Beetroot tumeric and pepper as her medication.

How To Training Manuals.

Body Piercing Basics

Body Piercing For Students

All the main points on body piercing.

Anatomy For Body Piercers

All Body Piercers should understand the body and how it works this is a wonderful tool for any Body Piercer.

Body Piercing Bible This book is having some major additions added to it and is off the shelf for now.

Eyelash Grafting Training Manual

Step by step instructions with video tutorials.

Body Piercing For Students

EyebrowsShaping & Tinting To Suit Face Shapes

Step by step instructions with video tutorials on eyebrow shaping, eyelash and brow tinting.

Cosmetic Tattoo Permanent Makeup Micro-pigmentation Training Manual

A step by step training manual. You could actually teach yourself the trade as this book is so well written.

An Angel For Cosmetic Tattooists

A helping hand for a cosmetic tattooist.

Hair Extensions Training Manual

Learn to create hair wefts, weaves, braids, wax in, and clip in Hair Extensions. There are videos to watch in the eBook.

Supernatural Books:-

Colours That Heal.

A breif to the point on colour s for power and healing.

Colours That Heal Version Two {To Be Released 2016}

Body Piercing For Students

 I may change the name of this book as I am writting it I am having some amazing input from someone out there in the higher world . It will be release some time this year 2015.

Spell Folklore

A great book on how to do some positive affirmations also called spells.

Tarot Scrolls 0-22

Ask a question open a page and an inspiring answer will be there for you to read.

<u>Children's Books:-</u>

Romeo and Juliette Keep Mark Antony

A wonderful story about a puppy born on a boat. His white cute and fluffy. True story with a dash of magic added.

Mark Antony Marries Lizy and Has Puppies

 Loaded with photos of all the dogs and the new born puppies. A true story with a dash of fantasy added.

 Authors website
http://www.beautyschoolbooks.com.au

email beautyschoolbooks@gmail.com

A WORD FROM THE AUTHOR.

Every year I try to release a book to help people do their hair and beauty treatment at home and books to assist those entering the hair, health and beauty industry. My own personal site will be up in July 2011 called www.beautyschoolbooks.com.au

Right now some books are on eBay at :-

beautyschoolbooks

and some on

http://www.thatsgreat.co

http://www.beautyschoolbooks.com.au

Other sites are Amazon, Smashwords, Barnes and Noble, Createspace.

Some of my you tube videos are:

Piercing
http://www.youtube.com/watch?v=gFzp9h
Sq8Cg&feature=related

Body Piercing For Students

Cosmetic tattoo machine

http://www.youtube.com/watch?v=wkQXs0ZXS18

ON YOUTUBE

I am placing a series of short to the point videos on YouTube next year 2016.

They are very homemade, videos are not my proficiency. But I am sure they will help the beginners.

Here are some to watch on my YouTube channel. The ones on piercing will naturally interest you the most.

Piercing How to Hold Forceps Eyebrow

http://www.youtube.com/watch?v=gFzp9hSq8Cg&feature=related

Navel set up

http://www.youtube.com/watch?v=Gzbs9hGJnk

Labret / Munroe

http://www.youtube.com/watch?v=hqzJjsFahqE

Body Piercing For Students

http://www.youtube.com/watch?v=kGcDY
Exsdg

About The Author

Her first ear piercing was on a friend when they were just twelve years old. Her best friends mum was rather impressed but when Robyna parents caught wind of this and they chastised her. The Author Robyna started her working life part time in a family salon in Kings Cross Sydney while still at school. Body Piercing although not popular in the 1950 here in Australia, it was very popular in Kings Cross Sydney. The methods of piercing have not changed much over the years but the dramatic changes have been to the industries health and safety regulations.

During School holidays and most afternoon from age five Robyna would help in the family Salon. By age, ten Robyna was performing the same duties of a 1st year apprentice. After her dancing lessons on a Saturday morning Robyna could not wait to get to the salon to help. Her father had jet

Body Piercing For Students

black curly hair and she would practice finger waving Saturday afternoons on his hair. He loved his hair being played with and would pay her threepence to place the wave clips in his hair. You could see a movie for sixpence in those days.

Robyna has won several major awards and was nominated "Business Women of the year." in 1987. As the owner of many salons Robyna has trained countless people in all facets of the Hairdressing and Beauty Therapy.

She studied

Hairdressing in the early 1960's at South Sydney Technical College.

Beauty Therapy with Madam Petrovic in Rose Bay Sydney. 1960's

Aromatherapy at Naturecare College in St Leonards.

To add to her credits Robyna was chosen in 1990s for the rewrite of the Australian Standards and again for the updates in 2007 to 2014.

Body Piercing For Students

Books By Robyna Smith-Keys are sold in many countries as well as on eBay in Australia these are the positive feedback from buyers.

☺	Excellent item, great value for money and super fast delivery, excellent A+	Buyer: 996
	Body Piercing National Training Course Manual Australia (#150667743741)	AU $39.50
☺	fast postage *very informative*	Buyer: dan
	Permanent Makeup Cosmetic Tattoo Training Manual CD (#150667681991)	AU $65.00
☺	this is so helpful ! i love it !	Buyer: wal
	Body Piercing National Training Course Manual Australia (#150661839803)	AU $33.50
☺	Thank you very happy with product and fast shipping	Buyer: cha
	Eyelash Extensions/Grafts Training Manual Revised April (#150657681811)	AU $33.95
☺	Thanks :)	Buyer: cha
	Body Piercing National Training Course Manual Australia (#150629313838)	AU $39.50
☺	very helpful ..thnx	Buyer: mk
	Eyelash Extensions/Grafts Training Manual Revised April (#150608377553)	AU $33.95

My students have all said the training manuals are to the point and very helpful.

The training manuals are tested on new students before the books are released. There would be no point in writing a training manual if it were not going to help students.

Body Piercing For Students

Within my 30 years of writing training manuals, I have only ever had one student say they could not make head or tail of what I was trying to teach her in the training manual.

I offered to go through the manual with her via Skype but she could not work out how to use Skype either.

With this in mind, I want you to know I am only ever an email away from helping you. You cannot always repay people for their amazing kindness but you can pass on their kindness. I want to pass on her kindness to you so feel free to contact me if you need to.

My email is:-
beautyschoolbooks@gmail.com

What is the difference of being trained under the international standards by a beauty industry professional?.

1. You can lean to pierce without anesthetics and still give a pain free piercing.

Body Piercing For Students

2. You will be more professional when trained under these codes. Because client care, such as taking their pulse, and checking on them a few days later.

3. Then cleaning the piercing within a week for them and reaffirming they are attending to their healing program correctly.

4. As a caring professional you can charge more for your service and clients that have had a piercing elsewhere, will experience and know the difference.

Should you need to do an online course then contact us at beautyschoolbooks@gmail.com

Happy Learning

~~~~~ *** ~~~~~

Made in the USA
Coppell, TX
03 September 2021

61739649R00138